The Laity and the Life of the Counsels

HANS URS VON BALTHASAR

The Laity and the Life of the Counsels

The Church's Mission in the World

TRANSLATED BY BRIAN MCNEIL, C.R.V.
WITH D. C. SCHINDLER

A COMMUNIO BOOK
IGNATIUS PRESS SAN FRANCISCO

Original German edition:
Gottbereites Leben: Der Laie und der Rätestand
Nachfolge Christi in der heutigen Welt

Cover by Roxanne Mei Lum

ISBN 0-89870-572-x
Library of Congress Control Number 2002113185
Printed in the United States of America ∞

CONTENTS

PART TWO: THE EVANGELICAL COUNSELS IN TODAY'S WORLD

ABOUT THIS BOOK

(Preface to the German edition)

The author had planned a new edition of his book *Der Laie und der Ordensstand* [The laity and the religious state] before his death, with the new title: *Der Laie und der Rätestand* [The laity and the state of the counsels] and the corresponding adjustments in the text. Carrying out his plan has given us the occasion to include in this publication some of his earlier writings about the layman in the Church, especially about the consecrated layman. These writings are now very difficult to obtain otherwise. We have given the publication [the German edition] a new title, which likewise comes from the author himself: *Gottbereites Leben* [A life held in readiness for God].

Der Laie und der Ordensstand appeared in 1948, in the place of the more comprehensive work *Christlicher Stand* [*The Christian State of Life*, 1983] (which was not made available for publication at that time),[1] immediately after *Das Herz der Welt* (1945) [*The Heart of the World*, 1979] and *Wahrheit I: Wahrheit der Welt* (1947) [*Truth, I: The Truth of the World*], as a third important accent in Hans

[1] On this, see Hans Urs von Balthasar, *Unser Auftrag* (Einsiedeln: Johannes Verlag, 1984), 83 [Eng. trans: *Our Task* (San Francisco: Ignatius Press/Communio Books, 1994), 99], and *Mein Werk: Durchblicke* (Einsiedeln and Freiburg: Johannes Verlag, 1990), 35 [Eng. trans.: *My Work: In Retrospect* (San Francisco: Ignatius Press/Communio Books, 1993), 43.—Ed.].

Urs von Balthasar's work, a kind of pointer to a possible answer man could make to this "heart" and this "truth". The following of Christ was and remained for him in all its forms a most profound concern, to which he returned again and again; it is an idea that conditions the totality of his mighty œuvre and gives it an ultimate pastoral orientation. A great inner joy streams out of these works, a deep love for reality: here a path emerges.

The essays have been included without any changes in their chronological order. Two later writings, scarcely known in the German-speaking world, form the introduction and the conclusion to this volume: *Gottbereites Leben: Über den Sinn des Rätelebens heute* [A life held in readiness for God: On the meaning of the life of the counsels today] (1971) and *Laienbewegungen in der Kirche* [Lay movements in the Church] (1987).

Since the ecclesiastical documents concerning secular institutes (*Provida Mater*, *Primo feliciter*, *Cum Sanctissimus*, and other texts in the selection made by Jean Beyer, S.J.) have been published [in German] as a separate volume by Johannes Verlag in 1963, we have omitted the appendix to the Herder edition of Der Laie und der Ordensstand (1949). The texts from the ecclesiastical documents quoted in that book have been replaced by the translation by Hans Urs von Balthasar in the 1963 volume. As far as possible, the notes to the essays have been brought up to date and expanded wherever necessary.

Despite a number of repetitions and thematic overlaps, which are scarcely avoidable in a publication of this kind, each of these essays contains a fullness of old and new insights; each has its own characteristic perspective on the one figure the author never wearied of contemplating: Jesus Christ, the one who calls us to follow him, who takes our following into his safekeeping, and who also makes it possible.

Feast of the Visitation of Our Lady, 1993

A LIFE HELD IN READINESS FOR GOD

ON THE MEANING OF THE CONSECRATED LIFE TODAY

1. "He called to himself those whom he wanted"

The starting point decides everything in advance. If we begin—as usually happens in the postconciliar period—with the Church as a fully established and organized people of God, articulated in its various functions, then we have already decided to a great extent the answer to the question of the function that the life according to the counsels has within the ecclesial fellowship. To be sure, this presupposition allows many possibilities for determining its function: for example, one can speak of making places of silence available, of specialists in spiritual counseling, of models of liturgical life for the parishes; at best, one can even speak of prayer on behalf of the brothers who are actively involved in the world and who have ever less time, and perhaps ever less inclination, to carry it out themselves—although mentioning this function of prayer in isolation from action in the world will run up against scepticism and resistance. Is prayer, especially "contemplative" prayer in its pure form, which would form the basic content of a life, a function within the Church, or is it not rather something alien from without (Neoplatonism, Stoicism, Asian religion), which invaded the Church at a later date and which has fallen behind the times, given recent reflection on the mutual compenetration of theory and praxis, indeed on the priority that praxis must have over theory for a Christian? Is it genuinely meaningful to seek God "in himself" as one who exists eternally and to make him the object of our lifelong contemplation and adoration, when God after all has emerged from within himself and wants to be "God with us": within history, sharing in suffering, sharing in the transformation of the world in view of a future that has not yet come? This question bores into the innermost core of the contemplative orders, creating an uncertainty, a disquiet that ultimately leads to a flight from the monastery into the Church's service of the world. Pure contemplation—if we wish to use this unbiblical word —threatens to forfeit its own self-understanding; all that remains for the life of the counsels are the functions mentioned above, in which they can continue to carry out a service that is useful to the ecclesial organism.

This is how things look the moment we take as our starting point the proposition that this social organism, this "people of God", is an adequate characterization of the Church. But the perspective shifts as soon as we recall that the term "people of God" is derived primarily from the Old Testament, so that it does not at all express the decisively *New Testament character of the Church*, which rather can be seen properly in the two terms "Body of Christ" and "Bride of Christ", both of which are closely linked to the mystery of the Eucharist: the Church becomes a body through sharing in the real, sacrificed flesh of Christ and in his blood that was shed—and this is not primarily an organizational, sociological "body", but a real "body" that is brought into existence through the Eucharist (1 Cor 10:16ff.). A little further reflection shows that it is only on the basis of the Eucharist that it is possible to conceive of the mystery whereby Christ the Bridegroom is "one flesh" with his Bride the Church (Eph 5:21ff.). Otherwise it would remain merely an edifying image, whereas for Paul it is the conjugal union that is the image, referring to the accomplished reality of the unification between Christ and the Church. One need not categorize the reality of the Church that lies in the terms "Body" and "Bride" as the "ontological" presupposition of the sociological level (Church as people of God); the word "ontological" is inappropriate here, because both descriptions possess an event-like character, just as both have to do with relationship; nevertheless, both descriptions, "Body" and "Bride", make it clear that in relation to Christ, the Church possesses no autonomy of such a nature that she could achieve in herself or—still less—on her own terms a self-understanding that would permit her to define and organize herself. To be sure, one cannot reduce the Church to the pure event of her springing forth continuously at every moment from Christ, thereby neglecting her relative position over against Christ (as a body stands over against the head, and the woman is over against the man in their being "one flesh"); but since this juxtaposition is never more than something relative, one may never detach it from the event of springing forth. It is not the case that Christ first forms a partner for himself, in order subsequently to communicate himself to her: rather, *in* his act of communicating himself, he creates his partner for himself, an extension of himself, "the fulness of him who fills all in all" (Eph 1:23).

Precisely at this point and in this context, we must recall that the Church does not emerge *en bloc* from her origin; rather, she is built upon apostles and prophets (Eph 2:20; 3:5). She does not in the least distribute these out of her own self: rather, they are the "foundation" upon which all distributions are able to follow. And just as the Church's ontic existence in herself is never able to catch up with the continually occurring event of her springing forth from Christ, so, too, the fact that she is constructed upon the "pillars" (Gal 2:9) that support her is never superseded but rather repeats itself explicitly again and again (cf. Rev 3:12); the calling of the Twelve, which derives totally from Jesus' own initiative (Mk 3:13), is only a foundational beginning; the concept of apostle is already broader than that of the "Twelve", for the case of Paul shows that there are new callings, new designations through the Holy Spirit (2 Tim 1:6ff.); these also include the prophets who are mentioned alongside the apostles in Ephesians 2:20 and the evangelists, pastors, and teachers mentioned alongside the apostles and prophets at Ephesians 4:11—all of these are designated for the formation of the members of the community and for services within it. We see clearly here that the exalted Christ has not at all abandoned his activity of calling people to the Church and for the Church. Just as it will never be possible for the Church herself to get a precise grasp of the relationship between the Church and Christ (to what extent is the Church Christ himself; to what extent does she derive her existence from him; to what extent does she stand over against him?), so it will never be possible to calculate exactly the relationship between those "called" and the rest of the Church: To what extent are they a part of the Church; to what extent are they, in their relative juxtaposition to it, the presupposition for the community's existence? At any rate, one may not think of the first reality without at the same time thinking of the second. Just as one may not consider ecclesiastical office in the postapostolic age as something bestowed by the Church, which "possesses" apostolic authority, so one may not reduce the ever-present event of the calling by Christ *for* the Church to a process that takes place completely within the Church, something that would lie completely under the control of the plans of the Church as "people of God". Just as office is established in her as an abiding and often uncomfortable sign of the fact that she does not belong to herself but to her Lord, so *spontaneous, free vocations that cannot be manipulated* are "instituted" within her by the Lord, which help her anew to achieve her own authentic "self-understanding", that is, to realize her dependence on the Lord and her task of leading her brothers in and outside the Church to him.

Despite this relative opposition, one must not make a sharp distinction between the immediate calling by the Lord for the Church and the articulation of charisms *within* the Church (which are likewise *for* the Church); there is a fluid boundary between these two events. But one must not overlook the point here that the charisms themselves are never "allotted" by the Church; rather, they are "assigned by God" to each individual (Rom 12:3) and realized by the Holy Spirit in keeping with his own free judgment (1 Cor 12:11), so that all the members of the Church share to some extent in the fundamental character of the "apostles and prophets", who are called specifically and in a qualitative way. Nevertheless, despite this inherent analogy, one cannot construct any egalitarian identity in the Church's structure. This is shown and guaranteed by the total expropriation of the "Twelve" and then of Paul and those who have to enter his expropriated form of existence through the "holy calling" (2 Tim 1:8; cf. Rom 1:1; Gal 1:15). While we cannot equate "office" and "the call by which election is made", both are spontaneous founding actions by Christ and, therefore, display a relatedness, indeed a mutual complementarity, since they both ensure that the "democratic" element in the Church remains bound to an antecedent fundamental personal element that makes it possible—and this is a principle that holds good right into the structure of the heavenly Jerusalem (Rev 21:10ff.).

2. *The Christological Foundation*

What has been said hitherto remains very formal, but it had to be said at the outset, in order to preserve for the life of the counsels a theological locus that would prevent it from being absorbed into a closed sociology of the Church. If the Church exists at each instant as something deriving from Christ, a reality that he entrusts to her, then nothing prevents this very formal element, which constitutes the Church, from being explicitly held up before her eyes again and again through the "office" and through the particular "calling". Being compelled to look upon herself in this particular mirror, she sees at each moment her own being and event as a whole. But how (we are speaking now thematically of "calling", no longer of the "office") is such an existence theologically possible at all? No doubt, it is possible by virtue of being ordered to Christ and being drawn into the act whereby his gift of self establishes the Church. But what act is this, and how is it possible to participate in it in a qualitatively special way?

The existential act of the Son is his *permitting himself* to be sent from the Father into human life and to be made incarnate by the Spirit in Mary's womb and then to behave in all the situations of his human life as the one *sent* by the Father, the one *made available* to the Spirit and *led* by him in his mission. The fundamental act of his existence is that he does, not his own will, but the *will of his Father*, and all his individual tasks are specifications of this fundamental act, all of what he does and what he refrains from doing, all his dealings with those around him, but also his suffering and dying. One can call this *fundamental act*, which is antecedent to all the individual actions and passions, his abandoning of himself to the Father's will, as this is made concrete and communicated to him in the Holy Spirit. Only this fundamental act supplies the key to the christological paradox that Jesus can appear with the highest claims and, at the same time, the greatest humility: where he apparently exalts himself in an inexplicable manner ("Who do you claim to be?", Jn 8:53), he is utter transparency ("My teaching is not mine", Jn 7:16); where the whole of his existence is taken up in an effort to allow God's Word in itself to become "flesh", it never points to its own self; rather it is "true" because it does not "seek its own glory" (Jn 7:18). Let us here note in parenthesis that the intermediate verse, 7:17, opens the possibility for others to enter into this form of existence and thus to test its truth from the inside; but first of all, we must draw another consequence, namely, that the Son's possibility of carrying out every human existential act as a function of his (active!) availability to the Father allows him to transcend the boundaries that are otherwise imposed on man: at the point where man himself fashions his decisions and works out of his own spontaneity, this spontaneity in Jesus (which is certainly present) is embraced and determined by his deeper gift of himself to the Father. And at the point where man's spontaneous working comes to its end, so that he must allow that which he does not want to befall him —opposition, suffering, dying, the experience that all he has done has been in vain, and so forth—this experience of boundaries, since it is accepted in the undiminished willingness to do the Father's will, is endowed with an equal, indeed, with an intensified "fruitfulness". The biblical word "fruitfulness" can be employed here, because it points beyond those expressions that have their validity in the active sphere where the world takes form: "intention", "goal", "achievement", "harvest", "success". What these words express can be measured—how many sick people have been healed, how much bread has been gathered together for the brethren, how many lonely old people have been cared for, and so forth—and this is precisely why it is finite, something that can be assessed and defined. But it is impossible in principle to assess and define and measure an unlimited availability, like that of the Son to the will of the Father, and for this reason there is no limit to the use the Father can make of it. This availability is the most precious material that can be offered to him—since it is not a resignation, but a love that is active and burning—and he can fashion whatever he wishes out of this material. Indeed, one must say that without this material, he could not form everything he wishes: for example, he would not be able "to reconcile the world to himself" by "making sin for our sake" the total loving willingness of the Son "who knew no sin" (2 Cor 5:19ff.), for this mysterious transfer on the Father's part needs precisely this boundless availability, that allows itself to be shaped into whatever the Father wishes. Otherwise, human plans and activities would always produce only finite human results (albeit good results pleasing to God), but never the kingdom of God. Finite human plans can make a contribution to the coming of this kingdom on the condition that they derive, not from the principle of one's own finite planning, but from the principle of perfect availability to the Father, in the Holy Spirit. Everything in Christ's existence is fruitful because, beyond all his own plans, he allows himself to be "planned" by the Father; he would never have been able to use himself so thoroughly as he is used and abused for the salvation of the world. For he would not have been permitted to take his own life (as the Jews suppose, Jn 8:22) for the sake of his brothers; such an act would have been of no use to anyone. Nor would he have been permitted to enter by himself into the experience of abandonment by the Father, for that would have meant setting limits to his love for the Father, or else discovering hidden limits that were already present, and once again, that would not have helped anyone. The decisive "actions" involved in the charge he has received can only be imposed on him by the Father, and naturally these could not have been imposed on anyone other than the one who makes known an infinite loving availability to the Father that allows the Father to do more with him than the Son himself would be able to do in his own power; this is the one a priori condition for the possibility of all the initiatives the Father takes for the reconciliation of the world. Thus, to take only one example, the lavish squandering of Jesus' existence to the whole world as Eucharist—flesh that is slaughtered, blood that is shed—is possible only because it is the *Father's* action that hands over the Son as the "bread of life", because the Son came from heaven, not to do his own will, "but the will of him who sent me" (Jn 6:35ff.). The Son's loving willingness to *let himself* be abandoned is no less infinite than the Father's loving willingness to save the world through the abandonment of the Son, and it is through the equally great readiness in the opposition of the one who sends and the one who is sent (within the unity of the Spirit, who carries it out) that God's plan can succeed. This one gesture of the triune God is his total, unsurpassable turning to the world; no individual Christian action directed to the world of his fellowmen deserves the term "Christian", and none is fruitful in keeping with the mind of Christ unless it is "built upon the foundation of Christ" (1 Cor 3:11).

3. The Life of the Counsels

But how is it possible for a finite man, who of himself is unable to posit any infinite acts tending toward God, to enter into the "form of Christ" in order to share in the fruitfulness of his work? The answer to this question has various levels: fundamentally, through faith, which renounces its own measure for truth and the judgment of truth and allows that to be true which is true for God; through baptism, in which he makes the gift of his own existence into the event of the death and Resurrection of Jesus and becomes a function of this event through God's act (Rom 6:3ff.); through sharing in the Eucharist, whereby he hands himself over in body and soul to the Lord, as a "member" of his Body, which is fruitful in its being distributed (1 Cor 6:13–20; 10:16ff.; 11:26; 12:12ff.). But, contrasting to some extent to this general answer, there is a second answer, which consists in the "life of the counsels", through which the act of self-expropriation in faith and of handing oneself over to God contains a completeness that cannot be surpassed by man himself. The first essential condition for this is that one can or may posit this act, not at his own disposal, but only on the basis of a particular *condition of being disposed of, being called, and receiving grace*; otherwise this act would contradict itself as soon as it was posited. For it is not seriously possible to have control over the state in which one is totally subject to control by God; all one can do—though consciously, in love, giving one's consent—is to *allow* oneself to be brought into this state. This insight forms the basis of the entire design of the Ignatian

Exercises. It is demonstrated through Mary's existence, with which the life of the New Covenant begins. Mary *is made* the mother of the Son in his Incarnation, and the grace bestowed on her makes her capable of uttering a boundless *fiat* to God, which is her fully activated faith (Lk 1:45; 11:28). This faith is offered, however, not in passive resignation, but with the active willingness of the "handmaid" for the action of the Holy Spirit, for something that she would never have been able to achieve by herself.

The Marian *availability* is so indivisible and comprehensive that it is pointless and impossible to distinguish within it the elements of virginity, of poverty, and of obedience. These are integrated in the fundamental act to the point of mutual compenetration, and they could be seen as individual elements only if one element were to be detached from the others and made the object of a reservation. Mary might, for example, have said: "God can have everything but my body", on the grounds that she was already promised to the man named Joseph; but she makes no such reservation. Just as it is unthinkable that the living corporeal-spiritual existence of Jesus could have been made available as bread for the world under the Father's hands if this existence had been bound elsewhere and made available in an earthly marriage bond, so it is at least in the highest degree "appropriate" that God should make use of a total human fruitfulness, unlimited by any tie, in order to let his Son become man: he makes use of the fruitfulness of a faith that places itself totally, body and soul, at the disposal of God's call and his word.

It is quite obvious that the way in which Mary holds

herself in readiness for God does not imply that "contemplation" predominates over "action" (if one has any wish to introduce here this pair of Greek categories that has no basis in the Bible) or that "turning to God" predominates over "turning to the world". She knows well enough, on the basis of her Old Testament religion, that the God of Israel is a "God with us" and "for us" and that he lays claim to a human being as his instrument only because he wants to carry out, through him, a saving deed for mankind. Knowing this, and trusting completely in God's plan of salvation, Mary unreservedly places herself in God's hands in order to put no hindrance in the way of his holiness ("in order to be holy both in body and in spirit", 1 Cor 7:34) and thus to permit God's work in the world to take place through her. In the *Magnificat*, she sees herself as given a clear place in this work: "For he who is mighty has done great things for me, and holy is his name. And his mercy is on those who fear him from generation to generation" (Lk 1:49–50). Thus the pair of categories mentioned above is utterly inappropriate to the act that lays the foundations of the life of the counsels. The concentration of a believing existence on the core of an existentially realized absolute availability to God is not contemplative, since nothing is "looked at" or "reflected upon": all that happens is that one makes what is one's own completely available. Nor is it active, in the human sense of this word, for nothing is undertaken in one's own power: all that happens is that one announces a fundamentally unlimited readiness. By the same token, this concentration cannot be called something "turned away from the world", for here a man offers himself for every work of the God who plans salvation: "Here am I! Send me" (Is 6:8); "Behold, I come to do your will, O God" (Ps 40:8 = Heb 10:7). Nor is this act simply "turned toward the world", for it is only through the will of the God who disposes over man that one turns to the world. What a mass of empty straw is threshed with these categories without finding any genuine wheat!

In comparison with what we have said here, the entire problematic concerning the life of the counsels that is discussed endlessly today is almost always secondary. If this were acknowledged and the validity of the primary principle admitted, then all the proposals for reform would be useful and salutary; but if one failed to understand the secondary importance of reforms, destructive forces would push their way into the Church's precious core, so that her innermost fruitfulness in God's work of grace would be struck. Instead of something that goes beyond what human power can achieve (what woman could give birth to a Son of God by her own power?), we would be left with a merely human, finite, problematical, and fragile power. Instead of a disposition to give oneself to God and allow oneself to be used by him for the world, we would find a turning to the world according to one's own criteria and discretion. Such an approach would of course believe it corresponded to God's intentions with the world, but it would not originate from the divine endeavor but rather from a place one had chosen oneself, that is, from one's own self. The true, illimitably fruitful strength of the Church would be abandoned and exchanged for short-winded individual actions, which often enough remain without success, thanks to the meager influence of politically and economically active Christians —and how many of these have professional qualifications in addition? For every Christian, whether he is a layman or a priest or lives in the life of the counsels, solidarity with the world is a natural task. Even the "purely contemplative Order" is no exception to this: rather, through the absence of special apostolic works, it allows the *fundamental Marian structure* of Christian readiness (which we set out above) to emerge into view in its purity. It may be true that earlier centuries did not think in a sufficiently biblical manner here and remained stuck within a philosophical-religious antithesis between God (as absolute) and the world (as relative); but we can supply the missing element today in such a way that the first starting point is not simply superseded. Even in Christian terms, "the gift of self to the absolute", "the absolute gift of self" (that is, the abandoning of a will of one's own that would lay down conditions for God), remains the presupposition for fruitfulness in the world, not out of man's capacities, but by the grace of the absolute God, who in his ultimate commitment to the world makes use of those who hold themselves in readiness for him. The reformed Carmel has understood perfectly well that such an offer to the living God means, on the one hand, following Christ in his Cross and abandonment and guarantees, on the other hand, in the most profound sense a fruitfulness in Church and world, although naturally the one who hands himself over will not be allowed to see on earth the fruits of his self-gift.

4. Distinguishing the Forms of Life

In relation to what has been said here, all questions about distinguishing between different forms of life in the counsels and about the concrete manner in which the counsels find expression in the conduct of life are completely secondary, no matter how difficult and complex they may be. The primary point is a *gift of one's life as a totality*, naturally after mature consideration and testing; but "temporary vows" contain a reservation that contradicts the fundamental act described above and that is therefore inadmissible. One who says that he cannot guarantee today what his decision will be in later years is confusing the abandonment of himself to God with an active, limited decision that the subject has to carry through out of his own strength; the same reasoning would compel us to speak of a "temporary baptism", a "temporary faith", and man would give a totally incommensurate response, indeed no response at all, to God's eschatological decision in favor of him. All the psychological objections must retreat here behind the clear theological demand. The vocational narratives of the Gospels speak an unmistakable language.

We have seen that the fundamental act that constitutes the life of the counsels is christologically determined; precisely for this reason, this act as such is higher than, and embraces, the tensions between turning to God and turning to the world, between contemplation and action, between acting and suffering. It is true that the Son's act is turned to God the Father in its fundamental dimension, but the Son knows that this is a Father who is resolved upon the reconciliation of the world and consequently upon the sending of the Son. But it is not yet established, when the Son looks up expectantly to the Father, how he will send the Son or how he will determine the individual phases of his life when the Son is sent; this will be revealed only when the Father makes his will known. This will be disclosed in such a way that some main articulations are clear to the Son once and for all, while the concrete directions to be executed are given only in each particular "hour" and situation. On the one hand, the fundamental readiness of the Son to do the Father's will must become incarnate anew in each limited empirical situation, in order to prove that it is an unlimited transcendental readiness; on the other hand, the individual act of execution may not for one moment be detached from this unlimited readiness and lay claim to a complete meaning in itself, since it has meaning only as evidence of the perpetual living presence of the continuous unlimited readiness.

If we wish to translate this into the Christian *life of the counsels*, then we see what norm must be heeded in the concrete shaping of the individual counsels. This norm will always be the same in all the different forms of the life of the counsels—from the cloistered contemplative monastery via the active orders and congregations to the secular institutes—namely, *readiness for total and unconditional availability*.

In the case of *virginity*, there can be no question about the unity of the norm in all concrete instances, especially when we look to the undivided bodily readiness of Christ to distribute himself in the Eucharist and to the equally undivided bodily readiness of Mary to become the fruitful womb for the Holy Spirit's work. In matters of *poverty*, the correct ordering—which can be regulated in quite varied ways in the different groups—must always be found in reflection on the christological norm: being content with what one is given, something that does not belong to oneself and must be used in keeping with the will of God. This means that one will always aim at a credible testimony to the fact that God himself became poor in order to make us rich (2 Cor 8:9): the Father became poor because he deprived himself of his only wealth, the Son, in order to bestow him on us; the Son became poor, because he has nowhere to lay his head other than the will of the Father, which expropriates him; the Spirit is poor, because he is the Spirit of the expropriated love of Father and Son, and his work consists in leading men's hearts from within (Rom 8:15f., 26) into the work of God's self-expropriation (Jn 16:13f.). This is why the truth of Christian poverty depends on the truth of the readiness to (ever new) expropriation, which is primarily a *letting oneself* be expropriated, and on the truth (which is recognizable and credible to the world) of the lived testimony to this interior attitude.

The reference back to the norm becomes hardest in the case of *obedience*. The Son looks continuously, ever anew to the Father in order to see the light of his will; many individual rays seem to unite in order to form the simple light: a total knowledge by the Son of the Father's basic attitude, an experience of life that both lies behind him and leads him onward, the directives of the Father's law, the prayers of the pious, the predictions of the prophets, but also the situation in which he finds himself and the men led to him by the Father (Jn 6:44), from whose pressure he must nevertheless often extricate himself, since the comprehensive plan takes priority over demands made by the immediate situation, even when this situation would apparently promise individual successes. It is the Holy Spirit who binds these multiple rays into a unity, who "remains [hovering] above him" (see Jn 1:32), continuing his role in the dispensation of salvation, the role he adopted at the Incarnation: since the Spirit "actively" carried out the Father's initiative through his overshadowing of Mary, while the Son "passively" *allowed himself* to be made incarnate (*incarnatus est*, not: *incarnavit se*). "The Spirit of the Lord rests on the one promised" (Is 11:2): in the Old Covenant he is always a Spirit who comes from above, guiding and inspiring, in sharp contradistinction to the false prophets' "own spirit" (Ezek 13:3). One of the ways in which it becomes clear that Jesus "follows" this Spirit and is "driven" by him (Lk 4:1, and so forth) is that, although the Spirit is granted to him in fullness (Jn 3:34); nevertheless, he does not have the Spirit at his *disposal* until he has accomplished his obedient work (Jn 7:39); only then, after he has been raised up, is he explicitly given the authority to have the Spirit at his disposal (Acts 2:33; cf. Rom 1:4).

The believer's readiness in the life of the counsels to join the Son in a total dependence on the will of the Father will consequently become concrete likewise as obedience to the Spirit who leads and drives him; it is the Spirit who mediates in the incarnate Son the immediacy to the Father at each individual moment and at the same time gathers together the scattered elements that go to make up the forming of decisions. But the driving Holy Spirit, whose "law" (Rom 8:2) the individual believer is to accomplish in obedience, is never bestowed on him otherwise than in the comprehensive bosom of the Church; only "together with all the saints" (Eph 3:18); it is not as an isolated individual that he is assured of that immediacy to the Father's will mediated by the Spirit, and this aspect of the Church that embraces him on all sides is made concrete for him in the rule, which is both spiritual and ecclesial ("approved"), and in the superior of the community, who embodies his incorporation into the Church's fellowship. This mode of participation in the immediacy of the Holy Spirit is the indispensable guarantee that the individual, who always remains a sinner (that is, inclined to put his own will in the place of God's will), does not confuse his own spirit with God's Spirit or simply equate his own spirit with the true spirit of the Church ("having this at his disposal"), perhaps fancying that he knows this spirit better than the Church's official representatives. Even occasionally necessary "protests" against certain forms and utterances of the Church can never take place prescinding from the common spirit of the Church, but only in an always ultimately obedient (if also full of tension) accord with the spirit of the Church, which is always also a hierarchically ordered Church. All this had to be said, or at least hinted at briefly, if we are to begin to see the rich variety of the forms of obedience in the life of the counsels.

At one end—that of the relatively "pure contemplation"—there is the total renunciation of any shaping of one's own life, in order to submit completely to the direction of a guide endowed with the Spirit, a "spiritual father" (abba); here, the abiding transcendent readiness for God is continually made visible in a straightforward way. Where the tasks that the Christian must accomplish in the world are more concrete, the integration becomes more complex: between the demands of the undertaken work, the will of the superior (who allows the comprehensive spirit of the community and of its rule, and ultimately of the Church, to become concrete) and the will of God in the Holy Spirit, which brings everything to unity. No matter how the elements are integrated, the following points will hold true in every case:

1. In the life of the counsels, the choice of a secular profession and the decision of whether to remain in or change it can only be a function and expression of the original (christological) readiness for whatever is God's will. This means that those decisions cannot take place through one's own initiative or independently of the ecclesial authority, which of course must pay heed here to the possible immediate directive of the Spirit to the individual (in his distribution of the charisms as he wills: 1 Cor 12:11). In the superior's and subordinate's common obedience to the Spirit, God's will can be discerned in such a way that the member does not lose his character as a member of the comprehensive totality and of its representation.

2. This will become clear for everyone (including those in the secular institutes) on condition that the urgency of the individual tasks in the world does not eclipse the fundamental christological form of obedience: the

individual task receives its particular Christian fruitfulness—precisely in the life of the counsels—by remaining, both as a whole and in the individual instance (at every moment), *an expression of absolute availability*. No task ever becomes the Christian's private possession. At any point in time, he could be called away in death; likewise, at any point he could be redirected by God. This does not mean that the will of an individual superior is directly identical with God's will, but it does at any rate mean that, when a new assessment is made, the interest and the good of the Church, as well as that of the community, including the superior's insight into what is spiritually good for the member, can take on decisive weight. If the original total availability is an act of believing love, and if the ecclesial integration takes place within the same selfless Christian love, then we have a guarantee that the *following of Christ* in his obedience to the Father through the Holy Spirit can succeed without disturbance and distortion.

3. The integration of obedience, as it is lived out concretely, into the all-embracing obedience of availability can take place variously at different levels, but this does not permit us to arrange the various forms within a hierarchy. Obedience in Carmel or in the Society of Jesus is not objectively "more perfect" than that in a secular institute, if the latter is understood in theologically correct terms and not watered down. It does not matter whether the rules provide that the individual details of daily work be laid down by the superior, or whether the superior possesses full authority to transfer a member without any great discussion from one position of responsibility to another, or whether a responsibility accepted in obedi-

ence has so much weight of its own that the superior (at least as an individual person), in assigning it, binds himself more profoundly as well and is therefore compelled to test his own concrete obedience to the Holy Spirit at a deeper level and to take this into consideration—the entire act of mediation always remains an actualization of the working of the Holy Spirit as the "rule" that the decreeing Father lays down for the Son who complies and for all those who wish to take on the *forma Christi* as the sole form of their life in the life of the counsels.

Since what is always involved here is the rule of the Spirit who was breathed out upon the Church at Easter and Pentecost, we stand a great distance from the Old Testament law. Rather, in the counsels of Christ we are not servants but sons; indeed, it is precisely by entering into his sovereignly free readiness for the Father that we are genuinely freed for the freedom of Christ and to become children of God. In the midst of our turning to the world, when we take on burdensome responsibility in the world, we are ultimately free in a free availability to God; we are not in thrall or subject to any worldly powers. Precisely in this way, we are able to commit ourselves to our task in a responsibility that is doubly fruitful: at the visible level, by attempting to carry out our task in Christian love for God and our neighbor, but more profoundly by *making ourselves available*—habitually and at every moment—to God in our task, in an ultimate act of surrender, together with Christ: how, when, where, and for as long as God wills.

PART ONE

THE LAYMAN AND THE LIFE OF THE COUNSELS

Prefatory Note

This short essay isolates a single problem from the great complex of questions concerning the Church's doctrine of the states of life. There is assuredly no part of dogmatics that is more neglected today than this one. Since the question touched on here is so urgent, I did not want to wait until I had completed a larger work on the entire doctrine of the states of life before publishing the present section.[1] As so often in Church history, ecclesial praxis has begun to anticipate and to supply a solution to that urgent situation before any theory or theology could do so: "Lex orandi lex credendi", "lex actionis lex contemplationis", so that the daring flights of thought are already superseded to a great extent by the daring flight of what has in fact been done. If the reader at some places senses the lack of a thorough justification of propositions and assertions that concern the doctrine of the states of life as a whole and in general terms, I ask him for the patience to wait for the next book,[2] in which I hope to supply what he is deprived of here. In the same way, I shall deal in detail elsewhere with communities of women, especially secular institutes of women. Let me finally observe

[1] On this, see Hans Urs von Balthasar, *Unser Auftrag* (Einsiedeln: Johannes Verlag, 1984), 83 [Eng. trans: *Our Task* (San Francisco: Ignatius Press/Communio Books, 1994), 99], and *Mein Werk: Durchblicke* (Einsiedeln and Freiburg: Johannes Verlag, 1990), 35 [Eng. trans.: *My Work: In Retrospect* (San Francisco: Ignatius Press/Communio Books, 1993), 43.—ED.].

[2] *Christlicher Stand*, 2d ed. (Einsiedeln: Johannes Verlag, 1977, 1981) [Eng. trans.: *The Christian State of Life* (San Francisco: Ignatius Press, 1988).—ED.]

that the critical starting point for this study was virtually a matter of chance and that the essential substance could also have been unfolded in an immediate and positive manner from the gospel and the emergence of Christianity; the critical part is in fact nothing more than a time-conditioned occasion for bringing to light the supratemporal significance this question has for the Church.

Hans Urs von Balthasar
Basel, Autumn 1947

Introduction

In the apostolic constitution *Provida Mater* (1947),[1] the Church has shown herself to be in truth a farseeing and provident mother. She has recognized a movement that has been growing for decades in most Catholic countries and has bestowed a clear outline on these formless, tentative efforts within various lay groups. This act signifies much more than a mere formal incorporation into canon law of the lay communities, similar to the religious Orders, which were coming into existence: it includes an endorsement of the idea of these communities as something corresponding to the mind and spirit of the Church, a gathering of their various approaches into a clear wholeness, a designation of a place for them within the forms of the states of life in the Church, and thereby, finally, an official legal sanction through the norms stated in the constitution itself and through the act of placing these "Secular Institutes" under the Congregation for Religious.

Thus, the Church has taken in this case a path opposite to that taken roughly twenty years ago, when she uttered her great pronouncements concerning "Catholic Action". Whereas those appeals came explicitly "from above", namely, from the Holy Father Pius XI in a very personal manner, and authoritatively laid down the form and the reform required to meet and satisfy an exceedingly urgent demand of the times, in *Provida Mater* a movement that explicitly arises "from below", from the bosom of

[1] For the text of the Constitution, see Jean Beyer, S.J., *Die kirchlichen Urkunden für die Weltgemeinschaften*, Der neue Weg, vol. 1 (Einsiedeln: Johannes Verlag, 1963); new translation by Hans Urs von Balthasar.

the people of the Church, is taken hold of and given its location in the framework of the visible ordering of the Church. The two movements meet in the middle, intersecting at a point, the determination of which appears to be a task of decisive significance for the contemporary structure of the Church. To be sure, we have not yet discovered all of the consequences that follow from the simple encounter of these two lines—neither the consequences that follow with necessity nor those that could be drawn in freedom.

"Catholic Action" shed light primarily on the relationship between the priestly state and the lay state, while *Provida Mater* sheds new light on the relationship between the lay state and the state of the counsels.[2] The intersection of these two yields a kind of fundamental unfolding of the problem of the states of life in the Church, a problem that may begin with very practical questions about the Church's situation today, but these lead back into more

[2] In keeping with the intention often expressed by the author of this work, the concept *Rätestand* (life of the counsels) is used here and in the following texts instead of the term *Ordensstand* (religious life), which was most frequently employed in the original edition.—Ed. The life of the counsels embraces all persons and communities that give their lives the form of the evangelical counsels of poverty, virginity, and obedience, to which they commit themselves in some way (public or private vows, an oath, a promise, forever or for a determined period). "Religious" in the narrower sense take public vows (solemn or simple), while members of lay associations, as these are understood and grouped together by *Provida Mater*, take only private vows or an oath or a promise. The usual concept that would include both groups would be that of the "state of perfection", but this is vulnerable to a number of misunderstandings—as if those who live in this state were personally perfect or as if perfection were attainable only in this state.

general views of the way in which the Church as a whole is built up through the states of life. When such vistas are opened up, vistas that are so vast and significant, we must all the more readily turn for help to the clear foundations of revelation and the great lines of the tradition of the Church's history, lest a sudden feeling of vertigo cause us to draw foolhardy conclusions. The light from these sources allows us to give a sure interpretation to the present day, even when this means that our eye cannot fully follow the perspectives that open up into the future. Nothing is more incalculable than the Holy Spirit, who blows where he wills; but nothing is more ecclesial and traditional, since "he will not speak on his own authority, but whatever he hears he will speak, and he will take what is mine and declare it to you" (Jn 16:13–14).

These views have always been contested by the Church and have been luminously refuted by Thomas Aquinas. Instead, one can use here the term "life of the counsels" (in a broadened sense), since what it involves for all its members is the embodiment of the three evangelical counsels within a community that expresses this state of life, while the form of the obligation can vary.

1. The Limitations of Catholic Action

"Catholic Action" was generated by the recognition that, "unfortunately, the clergy no longer suffice for the necessities and requirements of our time, either because there are too few priests present in certain places or because their voice and their exhortations no longer reach whole groups of people who consciously withdraw themselves from their influence. This is why it is necessary for all to become apostles, so that the world of the Catholic laity does not stand idly by but is closely united to the Church's hierarchy and to its directives and is present and involved in the sacred struggles, contributing its help, with the total gift of its person, through prayer and through the action it joyfully undertakes so that the faith may once again flourish and the moral life of the Church be renewed."[1]

This starting point contains two elements: first, the general observation that the laity should not "stand idly by" but ought to give their whole person in the apostolate. This observation is, ultimately, not restricted to the contemporary situation; it would have been obvious to a Christian of the first age and even to a medieval Christian. If it is or was no longer obvious to the modern Christian, this is clearly linked very closely to the second truth addressed in the Pope's appeal: the clergy is isolated, and this isolation goes hand in hand with the view that the clergy is the exclusively specialized organ for apostolic activity in the Church. Each of these truths reinforces the other: The more the Church "specializes"

[1] Pius XI to Cardinal Segura y Saens, November 6, 1929.

herself in the clergy, the more the layman leaves the responsibility for his apostolate to the clergy, and, thus in turn, the more isolated the clergy becomes from the rest of the world.

In the Church's first centuries, we find nothing that would correspond to such an isolation. The priests, although equipped from the very beginning with the threefold office, do not form a caste of their own in the secular sociological sense. Within the ecclesial community, the priest has a particular function, which is established by Christ and completely irreplaceable, but the effect is more to make visible the unity that arises among the community and all its members than to distinguish between "castes". "In the history of the priesthood from early Christianity until the high Middle Ages, we can follow the development of priesthood into a caste in the sociological and secular sense of this word. This process took many centuries, just like the reverse development of which we are still a part today. When the system of 'social castes' ceased, the priesthood, too, had to disappear as a caste in the secular sense of the word."[2] "To disappear" in the sense of no longer being an organic, complex whole within the secularized worldly society as it was in the caste-ordered society of the Middle Ages, but *not* to disappear insofar as the modern secularization of the structure of society has expelled the priestly group more and more from itself and has forced it to isolate itself increasingly into the unity of its group, almost of

[2] Paul Simon, *Das Priestertum als Stand und der Laie* (Salzburg: A. Pustet, 1930), 8.

its "caste". Paul Simon is correct to point out that the great Fathers of the Church such as Ambrose and Augustine "came from the general education of their period and thus could not lay claim to a special education as this was understood in medieval or modern theology". Ambrose had been a government official and had enjoyed a literary and philosophical education in keeping with his noble birth. In the same way, it was only gradually that the rhetorician Augustine grew into theology out of the philosophy and the intellectual attitude that were modern in his period.[3] The same is true of Clement and Origen, of the great Cappadocians, who acquired their first education at the university of Athens, and of Chrysostom, who suddenly found himself called to serve the Church after having likewise enjoyed the secular education of his age. Although this general education came to take on increasingly Christian and ecclesiastical forms in the Middle Ages and the early modern period, it is very important to note here that the educational path taken by the cleric was still a total path that included at least *in nuce* the entire knowledge available to that age; that the medieval university, while giving precedence to theology, was able, in view of the state of knowledge in the individual disciplines at that time, to communicate to each student, and especially to the theologian, a universal education that corresponded to its name; and that, in particular, it gave the theologian a kind of key position for all the faculties, which allowed him to contribute a decisive word to all their discussions. The first phase of secularization, the

[3] Ibid., 20–21.

Renaissance, did indeed shift the meaning of this central position away from theology and more to a general humanistic philosophy and education, but it did not essentially destroy the idea of universal education. But then —in a process that has not yet come to an end today— the specialization of all the areas of knowledge came increasingly into the foreground, so that the *optimum* of the "humanistic synthesis" had correspondingly to be lowered from the stage of maturity to that of youth, the only stage at which it was still possible to realize in essence and approach something like a *universitas litterarum*. One specialist stood alongside another, with ever less contact between them, and the priest, who had once had his secure position in the very center of the entire educational organism, found himself limited to one of many fields, stamped as a specialist for theology or for pastoral work. Theology for its part did not remain completely free from this universal trend toward specialization, since the new scholasticism developed more and more into a "scholasticism of scholasticism", and an ever greater number of subordinate disciplines of all kinds came to join the central disciplines in the education of the theologian, lengthening his study and the period of his education. While this gave the priest a more thorough training, it also made him take on more and more the color of the specialist. If one sets alongside this development the religious development of the modern period, which has led to a secularization of Christianity precisely in tandem with the secularization of the sciences, then two things become clear: first, that the priest is now seen as the "specialist in Christianity", so that the layman appears much more passive in the apostolate than in earlier ages; but second, that precisely this specialization weakens the priest's influence on the de-Christianized world and often enough makes it impossible. "For many people, even for believing Christians, [the Church] stands in this fluid life of work and of the economy in the same way as Sunday stands in the week, that is, it is an exception that has apparently or actually nothing to do with real life. The Church is the business of the clergy, who are paid for it. The priest can indeed make contact with real life, but he does so through tasks that do not belong directly to his ministry, whereas his own proper ministry characterizes him as a specialist who is responsible only for theological questions and for everything connected with liturgical worship."[4] But the more the priest becomes a religious specialist, the more the Catholic layman appears to him in turn as one who himself is a specialist in some secular field, a lawyer, doctor, technician, architect, editor, a man who knows his own field thoroughly and in all the questions that have to do with his field, including the so-called borderline questions, he has become more distrustful toward theologians' directives (and, indeed, the highest ecclesiastical positions are occupied by theologians and speak from a theological stance) than was the case in a period when a general humanistic education still existed. This attitude within the Church is only a quiet echo of the view that has become universal outside the Church: no one would allow the "religious specialists" —since their specialty, from the perspective of the sec-

[4] Ibid., 61–62.

ularized exact sciences and of economics, seems a somewhat comical affair—to tell them what to do.

"Catholic Action" was conceived on the basis of this situation: primarily to bridge the gap between the clergy, who represented the Church, and the secularized world outside, but secondarily also to bridge the gap within the Church between priest and layman. The essential point here is that Catholic Action in its original project was perceived as a kind of "extension" of the hierarchy into the world, allowing the official representatives of the Church, who were no longer in direct contact with the world, to make an approach to it through the mediation of the laity. Thus "Catholic Action" was defined as "the participation of the laity in the hierarchical apostolate of the Church".[5] This formula, whose wealth of meaning permits the most disparate interpretations, was first interpreted to mean that the layman received and carried out his apostolate in a kind of delegation from the clergy,[6] that the "Catholic Action" (of the laity) did not furnish directives (for example, the goals to be pursued) on the theoretical level but was an executive organ on the practical level[7] and that the layman was a kind of *causa instrumentalis* of the hierarchy—not a mechanical, lifeless

[5] Pius XI, handwritten letter to Cardinal Gasparri, January 21, 1927 (AAS 19, 45). Cf. ibid., June 29, 1931.

[6] "Above all, one should not forget that the laity receive their investiture from the ecclesiastical authority; they must look on themselves as the delegates and plenipotentiaries of this authority, in an activity that is an obligation for the lay people themselves": Msgr. Luigi Civardi, *Manuale di Azione Cattolica.*

[7] Letter of the Cardinal Secretary of State to the Italian bishops, October 2, 1922.

instrument, of course, but a living instrument rather in the manner in which the inspired authors of the sacred books with all their abilities were instruments of the Holy Spirit.[8] Thus, while the layman did receive responsibility, "in all circumstances the hierarchy retained the complete and final responsibility for the totality of Catholic Action."[9] Catholic Action was the "extension of the hierarchy" through the inclusion of the layman in Christ's one and only mission, which had been laid upon the hierarchy. This "is not to detract from the dignity of the layman"; on the contrary, "it implies an elevation, an honor, it is proof of the very great confidence that the Church has in the laity",[10] it was "the call to a service that is not far short of the priest's service",[11] participation in the bishop's preaching office[12] and in his pastoral office.[13]

One thing is clear: if the Action were truly to become something that engaged the specifically lay forces of the Church, then a purely external "delegation" by the hierarchy could not ensure it any sufficient foundation. This is why there was further reflection and then the discovery of the inner foundations—rooted first of all in baptism and confirmation, but also in the entire reality of the Mystical Body of Christ—for the laity's primary share in

[8] Dr. Michael Keller, *Katholische Aktion: Eine systematische Darstellung ihrer Idee*, published under the auspices of the bishop of Osnabrück (Paderborn: Schöningh, 1935), 63f.

[9] Ibid., 65.

[10] Ibid., 57–58.

[11] Pius XI to Cardinal van Roey, December 15, 1928.

[12] Leo XIII, encyclical *Sapientis*, January 10, 1890.

[13] Pius XI to Cardinal van Roey, December 15, 1928.

responsibility within the Church.[14] The idea of a "participation in the hierarchical priesthood" was sometimes almost wholly overshadowed by the idea of the "universal priesthood" of all the believers. Only thus did it seem possible to cut off at the roots the danger of clericalism, which Catholic Action was designed to abolish but which had not been genuinely overcome by the idea of a mere delegation to the laity. The one who went farthest in this direction was no doubt Ernst Michel, the spokesman for an ecclesiastical mission of the laity totally independent of the hierarchy. In his provocative book *Von der kirchlichen Sendung der Laien* (On the ecclesial mission of the laity),[15] he ironically describes the lay groups of the "Catholic Action" created by the clergy as a hybrid structure of modern clericalism, which sought in this way to break out of its ghetto but instead basically succeeded only in drawing the laity into the ghetto as well. As an alternative, he sketches out the sphere of the layman, cleanly separated from the sphere where the clergy work but equally essential: the autonomous and mature layman carries out the "secular office of the Church". The Church in her "pure form" (represented by the clergy), with no point of contact with the world, and the world in its pure form, with no point of contact with the Church, intersect in the layman, whose own responsibility it is, through moment-by-moment decisions, to create the synthesis. This means that he in fact stands at the most vibrant point of the Church, at the place

[14] For example, Rudolf Graber, *Die dogmatischen Grundlagen der Katholischen Aktion* (Augsburg: Haas und Grabherr, 1932).—Jürgensmeier, *Der mystische Leib Christi*, 6th ed. (1936).

[15] Berlin: Lambert Schneider, 1934.

wherein the lost world is transformed into the kingdom of God.

The advantage of Michel's one-sided program is that it exposes very clearly the inherent dialectic of "Catholic Action", which aims at the same time to overcome and to strengthen the clerical position in the Church and in the world: to overcome, by announcing the "maturity of the layman" and entrusting him with matters that apparently were hitherto reserved to the hierarchical ministry; and to strengthen, in that this maturity remains subordinate to the authority of the office both directly and indirectly, to such an extent that the laity are only "the executive organ" of the clerical program of pope, bishop, and parish priest. This is no merely theoretical dialectic, for it can be observed in a very real way within the Church, in an unmistakable lethargy and indifference on the part of the majority of the laity as soon as it is a question of joining any group of "Catholic Action" led by the clergy, indeed often with an ill-concealed resentment of the "organized power politics of the clergy", concerning which Michel makes no attempt to mince words. Many of the finest among the Catholic laity are frightened off and go their own private ways, "unorganized" and "unregistered".

The following reflection may help to uncover one of the reasons for this discontent. Everything that has been written about Catholic Action moves exclusively within the question of the relationship between the clergy and the laity and sees the salvation of the future Church as lying only in a new mutual relationship, a new movement that binds these two groups together. Nothing is more striking in this literature than the total absence of any mention of the third state of life in the Church, which is explicitly enumerated as such in the Church's book of canon law, for example, namely, the state of the counsels or "state of perfection". It is as if the state of the counsels had no existence at all in the eyes of Catholic Action. It is not mentioned in the official documents and is expressly excluded in many commentaries: "Those who carry out Catholic Action are the laity, that is, not the priests, and certainly not any members of the clergy or any members of Orders."[16] "Lay people in the sense of canon law are believers who have not received any ordination or who do not belong to any religious society. . . . Does this now mean that priests have no place in Catholic Action, that they stand as it were outside its sphere? Nothing would be farther from the truth."[17] But is there a place for religious? Once again, the question is not purely theoretical, for Catholic Action wishes to indicate the means that make possible an apostolate for the Church in keeping with the times, something (to put it even more fundamentally) that can ensure the survival of the Church within the secularized humanity of the future. The Church as a whole is at stake—to the extent that she is left to human care and planning. But the solution summons only two-thirds of the Church onto the scene.

And the solution is called "Catholic Action". Has sufficient attention been paid here to the fact that within the Church action and contemplation—and in another respect, action and passion—are correlative concepts? That

[16] M. Keller, *Katholische Aktion*, 31.
[17] Ibid., 83.

increased action demands increased contemplation and passion? That "Catholic Action" is possible only on the basis of deepened "Catholic contemplation"? It was a primally Catholic idea that led Teresa of Avila to set up the new Carmel as the first bulwark against the disaster of division in faith. And it is nothing but the simple gospel that lays down that when someone is sent out by the Lord into the world for a specific mission, for a special action, he must first take a radical leap out of the world, in order to gain an overview and distance and calm and depth in the detachment of contemplation, which can be given only by renunciation. In the Lord's life, thirty years of contemplation precede an action that lasts three years, and he begins these three years with forty days of fasting in the wilderness. From Damascus, Paul goes for three years to Arabia before he begins his apostolate. We hear the same about all the great apostles: each has his Manresa, his Cassiciacum, his Bethlehem, his Iris. This is part of the very law of Christianity's life. The one who wishes to speak must first listen; and in order to listen, he must become empty and still, *vacare Deo*, letting his ear deaden to the world's words and business, so that he can hear only God's word and God's business. Whoever wishes to enter into the world in order to be effective there in a fundamental way must first die to the world in a fundamental way. If one wishes to bring the kingdom of God "to all the peoples", like the apostles, he must first "leave all things", in order, being dispossessed of all things, to be able "to become all things to all men". There is nothing in the Gospels expressed more simply, more unmistakably, with a more timeless validity, than this law of the Christian's life. If the swing of the pendulum toward the world is to grow stronger, as "action", it must be balanced by the opposite swing toward God, as "contemplation", in such a way that the deeper contemplation precedes the deeper action as the enabling presupposition. And if this equilibrium is present, that is, if the apostolate is truly the imitation of Christ, then it will not be spared the Catholic passion. The apostle need not seek this specifically, unless as a voluntary penitence carried out for himself and for those entrusted to him; but he will see in this passion the confirmation that the sacrifice of his action was a fragrance pleasing to God.

Thus, if the Catholic layman is summoned forth today to a specific apostolate, it is essential that he also be given the possibility of finding in the *vacare Deo* the preconditions of his active mission. It would be an unpardonable error to locate the preparation for a decisive action merely in another "action", such as "effective job training", in busy-ness and mere organization. One often hears complaints about the sparse effect of the work that costs the parochial clergy so much energy in associations that follow the program of Catholic Action. There can be no doubt that one of the reasons for this disappointment lies in the fact that the law of action and contemplation does not find sufficient realization here. Are there not many parish priests and curates who have personal experience of this? They know the only means available to prevent them from sinking down into empty activism in all the busy life of the big city, in their own almost superhuman activity, is contemplation, to which they must hold inexorably fast. And if their state of life does not adequately guarantee them this means, would the first thing to do not be to return the state of life itself squarely within the axis of the Gospels through periods of relaxation, of contemplation, of prayerful recollection? A Catholic Action that disdained the law of contemplation would be in danger of becoming a kind of secularized pseudo-Order. Unconditional submission to the commanding organs, strict discipline, and immediate obedience in carrying out directives would be demanded, but the ultimate Christian meaning and spirit of obedience would remain alien to this organization—for this obedience is based exclusively in Christ's contemplative relationship to the Father.

If one looks realistically and plainly at the present situation, then it must be said that the discipline necessary has been attained only in the youth groups. Not only does the young person have more time than the working adult; he is also more easily guided, and this is not only because he is more capable of enthusiasm, but also because he has not yet made the decisive choice of his state of life and therefore possesses, as it were, latent possibilities that can later be developed only in the state of the counsels. But once the Christian layman has grown up, has established his own family and begun working,—and especially if he is an educated layman who would be particularly suited for a Catholic lay apostolate—then he stands almost completely beyond the formative influence of the clergy. All that remains is at best a very thin, sporadic "personal contact". Out of a thousand academically educated Catholics one will scarcely find five or ten who would be willing to join an apostolic association under the leadership of the clergy, in the spirit of the Action sketched by Pius XI.

Nor should one conceal from oneself the fact that an apostolate, in the full sense of the word, demands the whole man and thus the whole of his time. Apostolate in the full sense is not a hobby for one's spare time. But one cannot demand of the layman, who has a family and must care for them and earn their living, that he should make himself available with full commitment to yet another activity alongside his involvement with his family members and his profession. On the contrary, he will devote first of all to his family the slender amount of free time that he has left—and this will naturally include also the family's natural milieu, namely, relatives and friends. It is here that he will seek his relaxation; he will spend his holidays with them; he will look to the relationship with his wife for personal enrichment; he will devote his attention to bringing up his children; and apart from this, he will have precious little time for anything else. He will doubtless make use of the opportunities his job gives him for working as a Catholic, through the way he goes about his work and deals with other people. But he will not be able to make his entire existence an instrument of Catholic Action. Experience shows this to be true in the case of the average well-intentioned Catholic. It is indeed possible to apply to the (married) layman the concept of apostolate, that is, of an activity corresponding to the activity of the apostles, but in the same analogous (though indeed true) sense in which the concept of priesthood is applied to the (married) layman in the "universal priesthood of all believers". In order to become a priest in the specific sense, one needs an ordination and an office. In order to become an apostle in the specific sense, one needs a vocation to follow Christ in the sense of the apostles' "leaving all things", which is the presupposition of the total apostolate that is chosen as a form of life.

We can now conclude as follows: If the term "lay apostolate" really does express the demand of the present hour, but, on the other hand, the full apostolate demands the form of life of the counsels, then the concrete demand of the present hour is that we look directly to the synthesis between lay existence and the state of the counsels. *Provida Mater* has done this and has thus provided the most important complement to "Catholic Action". This complement was all the more desirable because, as we saw above, Catholic Action has hitherto left the forces of the life of the counsels unused. Indeed, it is not wrong to see a connection between this close link between secular clergy and laity, on the one hand, and the unmistakable tendencies, on the other hand, above all in France and Germany, not merely to ignore the state of the counsels, but to uproot it from its original significance. The school of the "spiritualité du clergé diocésain", which began with Cardinal Mercier and found expression in modern works by Masure, Thils, and Msgr. Guerry and in a writing like Msgr. Ancel's brochure aiming to attract candidates to the diocesan priesthood, attempts to absorb into the state of life of the secular priesthood the values proper to the state of the counsels, seeing in the latter nothing more than certain forms of a more private self-sanctification that have come into being in the course of Church history and that are therefore not ultimately evangelical but ought to be redirected or even abolished. This widespread way of looking at things leads the clergy more and more strongly to shift the structure of the Church into a mere co-existence of ecclesiastical office and parish, thereby excluding the state of the counsels from this essential structure. Many bishops say openly today that they see religious priests as an important and welcome help for regular parochial pastoral work, which is still indispensable today, but that a further development of the clergy could one day make religious priests superfluous. Against this, it can be seen that the mere polarity of clergy and laity will always encounter at some point the theoretical and practical limits of a "dialectic of clericalism" (and, correspondingly, of laicism) if one overlooks the third, fecundating, widening, and liberating element of the "evangelical life" in keeping with the Church's almost two thousand years of tradition. What is involved is thus not at all an either/or between "Catholic Action" and the idea of the counsels, between *Ubi Arcano* and *Provida Mater.* Rather, it is a question of making the idea of "Catholic Action" ultimately possible and fruitful through the idea of the total imitation of Christ, of seizing the point of intersection from which it is possible to release the Church's as yet undreamed-of forces for her apostolate, for her working in the world.

This is especially true in view of the situation confronting the Church today, with the advance against the West, against Rome, of the Iron Curtain, behind which the Church as a clerical institution is being mercilessly destroyed. "Catholic Action", as it was planned, presupposes a calm and secure collaboration between clergy and laity. The only form of "Catholic Action" that may perhaps in a short time still be possible could be an action of the laity who have been compulsorily promoted to maturity through the decimation of the clergy. Only if these lay people, having made themselves available for the work of Christ in the undivided totality of their existence, present themselves as ready in the midst of a totally secularized and God-forsaken world may we have hope that the Church will survive the onslaught in the countries that have been overrun. But the married layman, who is essentially "divided" according to Paul's words (1 Cor 7:33), will be able to acquire such an undividedness only with difficulty. He will indeed make an irreplaceable contribution in his job, in the organized cell of the family and his circle of friends. But if the apostolate in the great Pauline sense is to find embodiment, we will need people who are totally free for the service of the gospel, even in the midst of the world and of their work.

2. *The Lesson of History*

As theologians see it,[1] Christ brought the state of the counsels and the priesthood together in the person of the apostles. A certain amount of subsequent reflection on the part of the Church was needed before the radicality of following Christ by "leaving all things" could be separated from the office of priesthood; this reflection did indeed have certain beginnings in the gospel, but it could not be made explicit from the outset. For one thing, the state of the perfect following of Christ had been opened up to women as well, while office was

[1] Cf. Suarez, *De religione*, bk. 3, chap. 2, no. 3; *Opera* (Vives) 15:231.

reserved to men. Moreover, it is at least doubtful, in the case of some of those whom the Lord called to follow him (such as the rich young man), whether this meant that they were called to the priesthood, too. The evangelical counsels are addressed to all, and their path lies open for all those who can understand it. The first in the community to choose these counsels as their form of life were lay people: virgins and so-called ascetics. But even before these emerged as a clearly delineated group, the early Church already experienced a fruitful tension between those entrusted with an office and those with a charismatic commission, between designated "teachers" and "prophets" sent by the Holy Spirit: the fact that the latter's mission had to undergo an official testing and discernment of the spirits does not mean that it was itself an official hierarchical mission. As early as Paul, we see that the Church was founded on apostles and prophets, on office and charism (Eph 2:20; 3:5; 4:11). Thus there existed from the outset a distinction between those who bore the hierarchical office, with its objective perfection in teaching and the administration of the sacraments, and bearers of personal charisms, who were called to subjective perfection in the utterly total imitation of Christ. As soon as the early Christian eschatological ideal of holiness in martyrdom, in which both forms meet, faded into the background, the laity took the lead in the state of personal, subjective imitation, although no noticeable tension between the two states was introduced. The personal union of the two in the apostles continued to have such a strong influence that the great representatives of office took it for granted that they should bestow on the objective holiness of the office the subjective expression of "asceticism". The great Fathers of the Church were all either ascetics and monks themselves or else enthusiastic promoters of the life of perfection.[2] Nevertheless, the actual development of the state of the counsels took place through the laity. It was they who were the first to portray through their own life the Lord's forty days of fasting in the wilderness, to embody his perfect obedience to the Father in an incarnated, sociological form vis-à-vis the superior installed by God, and to choose the virginity of Christ and of Mary as the form of their own fruitfulness for God and the Church. It would be easy to show how the idea of the perfect gift of self and the personal consecration of one's life dominated from the very beginning all those who chose the state of the counsels as *therapeutæ*, ascetics, virgins, and monks, and thus how

[2] To give only a brief overview: some "ascetics" (before the foundation of monasteries with rules) who would certainly have become "monks" a hundred years later are: Justin, Tertullian, Clement, Origen, and doubtless also some of the apologists. "Monks" before their ordination to the priesthood or episcopate: Chrysostom, Basil, Gregory Nazianzen, Gregory of Nyssa, Epiphanius, Jerome, Paulinus of Nola, Augustine, Rufinus, Serapion of Thmuis, Diadochus of Photike, Salvian, Faustus of Riez, Gregory the Great, Cassian. Decisively important promoters of monasticism (or at least of the ideal of virginity): Methodius, Athanasius (with his epoch-making Life of St. Anthony), Cyprian, Ambrose. Attempts to give the clergy the monastic ideal as their form of life were made above all by: Eusebius of Vercelli, Ambrose, Augustine. Purely monastic theologians are, *inter alia*: Didymus, Evagrius, Isidore of Pelusium, Ephraem, Vincent of Lerins, Leontius, Sophronius, John Moschus, Maximus the Confessor, John Damascene, and assuredly also Dionysius the Areopagite. On the other hand, of the Church Fathers who thought and worked above all as priests we could mention: Irenaeus, both Cyrils, and Leo the Great.

the way in which this gift of self was made explicit in the three vows of poverty, virginity, and obedience in the eleventh or twelfth century was nothing but an unfolding of something that had always been present in embryo. These vows are contained in the state of the counsels in the first centuries just as truly as the seven sacraments are contained in the pre-Nicene, indeed, in prescholastic theology. Just as the rites and customs of the administration of the sacraments have been subject to many variations in the course of time without their essential core being affected thereby, so the forms and customs of the life of the counsels have varied in the course of Church history without the clear substance of the state of the counsels being in the least affected by this or drawn into the flux of changes. This is why Thomas Aquinas emphatically rejected a merely "material" understanding of the three fundamental vows—as if it were possible for other vows or counsels, perhaps an arbitrarily chosen number, to stand alongside these as equal in value. Rather, he saw in them the formal expression of the essence of the perfect following of Christ as a state of life.[3] And the Church will no more depart from this than she will depart from the sevenfold number of sacraments.

Two things characterize this state of being called to a particular following of the Lord. First of all—in contrast to office as objective holiness—it is the special state of life of subjective holiness, which, since holiness can of course never be a finished quality or an accomplished goal, remains here below always something in the process of

[3] St. Thomas Aquinas, *Summa theol.* II-II, q. 186, a. 7.

coming into being: *status perfectionis acquirendæ*. But since all holiness in the Church is a sharing in the Church's own holiness and thus a social holiness, it holds true in the state of the counsels that the one who takes the special path of holiness will ultimately seek this, not for himself, but for the Church, and the Church will always look on him in this sense as a member, a realization of *her own* holiness. No one in the Church is holy for himself alone, since Christ's holiness essentially consists in the fact that he sanctifies himself, that is to say, sacrifices himself, *in order that* others may be sanctified, that is to say sacrificed, in the truth (Jn 17:19). No one can make the gift of his life in poverty, chastity, and obedience in order to win it back for himself, since the Lord makes the gift of his life for his sheep (Jn 10:11), for his friends (Jn 15:13), for us (1 Jn 3:16). Thus it is impossible to understand the fruitfulness of the sacrifice in the state of the counsels except as something ecclesial or to understand the effect of this imitation except as something apostolic, irrespective of whether this apostolate is carried out more in action or more in contemplation. The first centuries are already perfectly aware of this—one need only read the life of Saint Anthony, as Athanasius narrates it, to perceive this: for although the idea of the ecclesial fruitfulness of the sacrifice (like so many other ideas at that period) remains implicit, it is there, and it makes its presence felt. Precisely in the wilderness, Anthony is *the* confessor of Christendom; precisely on the pillar, Simeon Stylites is the beacon summoning the masses to conversion. This is how things will remain until Brother Klaus, until Charles de Foucauld.

Now, nothing could be more important today than casting the brightest possible light on this social function of Christian holiness and perfection. It would put an end to all the widespread mistrust of the evangelical counsels today, and thus it would most importantly make it possible for the flame of the gospel to flare up again in its original purity and its consuming power. It is clear that as long as the ideal of holiness is laid down in individualistic terms (as it is to a large extent in scholasticism and in baroque theology), as long as it is a question of "my" holiness, "my" perfection, "my" virtue, then—even if they happen to be excellent educational instruments—the counsels would have to be judged as fundamentally negative. For the "values" of the spirit (self-determination), of the body (fruitfulness), and of the ordering of worldly goods belong to the "I" that wishes to achieve something in the realm of holiness. To renounce these values means fundamentally, on the worldly and natural level, renouncing precisely that "I" for which the individualist strives on a higher level, the "I" to which he wishes to hold at all costs. This is why the counsels appear to him something negative, a *fuga sæculi*, flight from the world, and, precisely for this reason—because of course something negative can never be one's goal—only a secondary means (*secundario et instrumentaliter*) toward the primary goal, namely, "perfection". But what saint—and thus we can say: what Christian—will aim at *his own* perfection as his goal? Is not his goal God, whom he loves, and the neighbor, in whom he recognizes God? And will he not fling himself directly into the arms of this goal, without reflecting much on his own self? What man, standing by the lake on a hot day and wanting to bathe, would find the impatient stripping of his clothes to be something "negative"? And when did the gifts that one gives one's beloved in love become something negative? They would be negative only if the giver were a calculating miser who felt that every gift was something painfully stolen from himself. But what would then become of the love that that theology portrays as the "primary goal of perfection"? The theology of the evangelical counsels that is common coin in the Church even today has a clearly individualist, bourgeois flavor to it (and one must of course ask whether the theology of marriage and of the state of life in the world does not suffer from the same sickness). This situation will not improve until the decision is made to abandon the ideal of spiritual self-development and perfecting, the religious "ideal of the personality", in favor of an ideal of being free for Christian *mission*, which never coincides with the personality of the one sent, or derives from it, but lays claim to everything in the person—possessions, body, and soul—in order to be able to make him in all respects God's messenger in the world. The one who finds in mission his wealth, his fruitfulness, and his freedom—in these three things, God gives him a share in his divine goods—can no longer see something negative in the living out of the counsels. For him, the counsel is no longer primarily a "means" but rather the "expression" of love (*perfectionis effectus et signa*: Thomas, *Contra Gent.* 3, 131).

The second characteristic of this life is its origin, which is constantly new, as it is born of the Holy Spirit. The Orders, the strongest bulwark of the Christian life in the Church, are perhaps the only thing in the Church that she herself has never founded: each time, she has received them anew from above, from the Holy Spirit. Not only this; in order to make known the purely supernatural character of the foundation, the Holy Spirit almost always chooses people who, considered according to external criteria, do not seem at all suited for such an office—nor do these people think in any way of founding anything, until, from outside, they are inexorably led along the path that God has prepared for them. Many go into solitude, perhaps unconsciously imitating Jonah's flight from the divine Spirit, until they are surprised precisely there and become the fathers of a first community almost against their own will. Others begin to gather companions around themselves, still without any firm idea of the form the community will take. They know only one thing, that God wants it. They are prepared, along twisting pathways that they themselves cannot comprehend, for a mission that may perhaps come only later, for the infusing of the new spirit they are to inspire through the mediation of their spiritual family and the Church. God confronts them with a fait accompli, and they in their turn confront the Church with a fait accompli. Their human nature serves at most as a resource, never as an exhaustive explanation, for the new direction, the new spirit, the new charism that they are to plant in the Church. Thus they fall into the garden of the Church like a meteor, and although the Church will assuredly test the claim that they make (for otherwise she would be neglecting to carry out her office), she does not possess the right to reject or suppress such a mission once it is recognized as divine. For this is precisely the language the Holy Spirit uses to speak to her through the centuries, concretely and unmistakably indicating to her in these figures the tasks of each age of the Church and the paths to their solution. Their position is like that of John, who conveys and interprets the presence and the will of the Lord to Peter at the Last Supper and later by the Lake of Tiberias, while Peter gladly lends him his ear. The ecclesiastical office has never at any time founded Orders; it can issue directives, and it can organize, thereby initiating certain currents and movements. The founding of Orders and communities that personify a new or a renewed spirituality in the Church stems originally from the Holy Spirit, who usually makes use of humble lay people in this work. Through all the centuries, the movement to the "life of perfection" or "state of perfection", to the evangelical imitation of Christ, has been primarily a lay movement. The subsequent "clericalization" of many great Orders did not correspond to the original intention of the founders but arose through certain later adaptations and necessities.

Thus the whole of monastic life before Benedict, the monastic world of Egypt, of Syria, and of Palestine, was a lay world: it was indeed in close contact with the clergy, but was cleanly separated from the clerical world. Basil, too, founded his Order, not as priest and bishop, but as a monk, and he wrote the Rules before his priestly ordination. Just as there were a few priests in the monastic communities that existed before his time, for the liturgy and the administration of the sacraments, so Basil, too, laid down that each monastery should have a couple of priests; but the real body of the monks consisted of laymen who were handworkers and farmers, people who also looked after the poor and the sick and did not live in any very strict seclusion from the world. Benedict, too, was most probably a layman, who opened the doors of his monastery to laymen, and the hierarchy of the monastery up to the abbot was a hierarchy of laymen; rank, unless determined by the offices held in the monastery, was decided by the date of profession.[4] A long time passed before this situation changed, and the number of the

[4] Benedict was cautious, almost suspicious in the matter of receiving priests who were not designated as such by the abbot but who knocked at his monastery doors with an ordination they had received in the world: "If a priest requests to be received into the monastery, one should not grant his request at once. But if he persists in his desire, let him know that he must observe the rule in all its strictness, and no concession will be made to him; the words of Scripture apply here: 'Friend, why have you come?' " (Rule, 60; cf. Balthasar, *Die großen Ordensregeln* [1948], 204ff.). He may exercise his priestly functions only if, and to the extent that, the abbot permits him to do so. In keeping with the dignity of his office, his seat is immediately after the abbot's; but when it is a question of filling an office or some other matter affecting the monastery, "then let him take the place that is his according to the date of his entry in the monastery, not the place that is granted him in view of his priestly dignity" (ibid.), "in order", as Ildefons Herwegen comments, "that his ecclesiastical position may not bring any pressure to bear on the others in significant decisions that affect the good of the entire community" (*Sinn und Geist der Benediktinerregel* [1944], 356). Chapter 62 of the Rule begins: "If the abbot wishes to have a priest or deacon ordained, let him choose among his monks one who is worthy to administer the priestly office. Let the one ordained guard against arrogance and pride; let him not presume to do anything without the permission of the abbot; and let him know that from now on he must submit himself to the monastic rule more than ever. . . . Let him always take the place that is his according to his entry to the monastery" (Rule, 206). Thus it is the abbot, who can

priests increased. "The reason that monks began to be incorporated increasingly into the ecclesiastical hierarchy is because of the missionary work of the Benedictine monasteries" and also because of the "necessity of pastoral work among those who lived in the countryside". "It is possible to some extent to check the numerical proportions between the clerical and the lay monks from some lists of members that have survived. Here we see that, at the end of the eighth century, the lay monks and those in minor orders still formed the overwhelming majority. In Salzburg in the year 784, for example, out of ninety-seven monks, twenty-two were priests and nine were deacons or

---

be a layman, who determines who will become a priest and who is worthy of it; the priesthood remains totally integrated into the monastic form of life and fulfills a "function" in the community of monks. The one among the monks who is a priest is to be distinguished from the others by greater humility and submission to the rule (Rule, 60). Herwegen praises the harmonious balance that was found between an official hierarchy and a pneumatic hierarchy after many centuries of struggle (*Sinn und Geist*, 362–68). But this balance holds good only within the monastic ordering, in which the state of life grounded in an official function must be subordinate to the state of life grounded on a total form of life. Abbot Leodegar Hunkeler summarizes it well: "The priesthood is indeed higher and holier in terms of ordination; but in terms of vocation the priest-monk is first of all a monk, and the exercise of his priesthood is bound to the limits that are drawn for him by monastic life" (*Vom Mönchtum des hl. Benedikt* [1947], 29). More recent attempts in particular Benedictine abbeys deliberately to restrict the number of the priests and to reestablish the idea of the "pneumatic hierarchy" have so far been perhaps a little too historicizing to be fully convincing. Nevertheless, we should not close the path to possible further developments in this respect. German plans from the prewar period, for example for a monastic community of lay theologians and lay scholars on a Benedictine basis, would be worth a fresh look.

subdeacons. In Moosburg, of seventy-one monks, twenty-two were priests and six deacons. In the first half of the ninth century, however, the lay monks and those in minor orders were already in the minority, that is, still about forty percent; in the tenth century, they sank to about a quarter of the total. At the beginning of the ninth century, the number of priests represented something under a quarter or sometimes even less."[5] It is nevertheless very significant that this development would not at all have led to the relationship that now exists between "monks" and "lay brothers" unless a second change had taken place, namely, the incorporation into the monastic community of servants, serfs, and farm workers, who initially had worked in the monastery as secular laymen. First in Hirsau and soon thereafter in Cluny, these, too, made their profession as genuine religious brothers, from then on forming the group of "lay brothers" who could never become clerics, a kind of subordinate category of religious under the choir monks, who were priests.[6] "From this point on, the members of the Order were distinguished into two groups: the monks (later called capitulars and conventuals) who belonged to the clerical state, who had the obligation of service in the choir and who were normally the only ones who could attain the higher offices in the monastery; and, on the other hand, the lay brothers (converses) who carried out only physical tasks usually had neither active nor passive voice in elections, nor . . .

[5] Philibert Schmitz, O.S.B., *Geschichte des Benediktinerordens*, German trans. Father Ludwig Räber, vol. 1 (Einsiedeln: Benziger, 1947), 253.

[6] Ibid., 255.

did they belong to the clerical state."[7] Thus this clericalization of the Benedictine Order (as well as of those that issued from it: the Camaldolese, the Vallombrosians, the Grandmontians, and the Cistercians) divided the religious community into two sections: one clerical, with a correspondingly higher education and holding the spiritual offices, and the other lay, with a low education and in an explicit position of service.

A similar shift can also be observed in the founding of Francis of Assisi's Order, which was initially wholly lay. His disciples were meant to be laymen, portraying the perfect life of the poor Christ in the midst of the world through their penitence, their prayer, and their preaching.[8] After the resignation of Saint Francis' first successor, the layman John Parenti, who had earlier been a lawyer, Brother Elias of Cortona, one of the founder's first disciples and once again a layman, became General; but he gave such preference to the lay brothers, who were more acquiescent instruments in his hands than the clerics,[9] that he had to be deposed at the General Chapter in Rome (1239). His successor,

> Albert of Pisa, was the first General of the Order to be a priest, and no layman has been General since then. The presumption of the lay brothers, who had been given excessively favorable treatment after Elias became General, went to such lengths that Haymo of Faversham, the suc-

[7] Max Josef Heimbucher, *Die Orden und Kongregationen der katholischen Kirche*, 3d ed. (1933), 1:204–7.

[8] Walter Nigg, *Große Heilige* (1947), 52–62, is correct to point out emphatically the nonmonastic character of the Franciscan foundations.

[9] Heribert Holzapfel, *Handbuch der Geschichte des Franziskanerordens* (Freiburg: Herder, 1909), 26.

> cessor of Albert (who died as early as 1240), excluded the laity completely from offices in the Order and recommended that the reception of laymen into the Order be numerically restricted. This seems to indicate that, at that period, the clerics were certainly in the position of moral superiority, though not of numerical majority, for otherwise it would have been difficult to carry out this resolution.[10]

Elias was later excommunicated by the pope and excluded from the Order. In the view of Father Holzapfel, the change that came about around 1240, less than a quarter century after the death of the founder,

> was, moreover, not in the least contrary to the Rule and had to come about gradually, since the priests had become ever more numerous, and the superiors of the Order themselves were allowed to exercise the care of souls vis-à-vis their subordinates. But we often find cases later on in which lay brothers were entrusted with offices in the Order if they had the necessary education. One should never forget that the *fratres laici* of the first centuries cannot simply be equated with today's brothers, who have the practical business of running the houses. *Clerici* and *laici* today are distinguished not only through ordination, but also through the level of their education; however, this was by no means always the case earlier on. Scholars, lawyers, doctors, and so forth, who entered the Order did not always receive ordination; thus, they remained laymen, although they might well have had an education and an ability for government superior to that of the clerics.[11]

[10] Ibid., 28.
[11] Ibid., 174–75.

This significant testimony shows that the clericalization of the Franciscan Order took place in a manner similar to that of the Benedictine Order, although certainly not for the same reason. The effect in both cases was the same: the separation between an educated stratum of priests and a subordinate, uneducated stratum of laymen. In 1260, under the generalate of Bonaventure, it was laid down once again in the Constitutions of Narbonne: "Lay brothers for domestic service are to be received only in situations of necessity and with the special permission of the General." The reform movement that began in Italy after 1400 initially gave rise to monasteries consisting primarily of lay brothers, but this changed again very quickly, when famous priests and preachers, like Bernardine of Siena, joined the movement. Persistent endeavors on the part of the lay brothers over the centuries to receive office in the Order,[12] viewed generally, came to nothing.

The Dominican Order was founded as a priestly Order. This makes sense insofar as the aim of the Order, the defense of the faith, could be achieved only through educated members, and education was to a large extent the privilege of the clergy. The monasteries, which were the heirs of the classical school in the early Middle Ages, handed their privilege to the universities in the thirteenth century, and those who studied at the universities were called *clerici*, a word applying to all who aimed at academic education. (The French and English words "clerc"/"clerk" have transmitted this meaning in part down to the present time.) "The *clericus* was a partic-

[12] Ibid., 459–60; cf. 202, 604, 629–30.

ular type, separate as a social group from all other groups such as the knights or artisans, and so on. He represented the education to which the knight, for example, did not aspire and, in fact, rejected as something harmful and unworthy of his social group."[13] "All education at this period came from clerically organized institutions, and all who sought academic education began by attending the general philosophical school of the period, sharing in the metaphysical questions posed by this period and making their own the answers given by scholarship. The lawyer and the doctor spoke the same language as the philosopher and the theologian." But it was only the theologian who possessed the totality of knowledge. The assurance of a livelihood necessary for education, which the monastery had provided at an earlier period, was given in the corporation of the university through grants and stipends, with the consequence that very many men forced their way into the station of the cleric although they had no vocation to the priesthood or to religious life. The clerical class of the Middle Ages was not at all identical with that of the priest as pastor or celebrator of the liturgy, and membership in this class did not as yet imply any definitive obligation, but only an orientation toward the priesthood.[14] Mandonnet writes in his book about Dante: "Being literate means being a cleric, and being illiterate means being a layman", and he quotes some words of John Balbi from Genoa: "Laicus, id est extraneus a

[13] Paul Simon, *Das Priestertum als Stand und der Laie* (Salzburg: A. Pustet, 1930), 38–39.

[14] Ibid., 42–43.

scientia litterarum."[15] This entirely explains why an apostolic Order for preaching and the defense of the faith at that period had to be composed of clerics.

Although this meant the frustration of the original conception that the great founders Benedict and Francis had of the state of the counsels, according to which laymen could form together an autonomous community even of a hierarchical character, or at least priests and laymen could live together under the perspective of the state of the counsels in complete equality of rank and of rights, nevertheless there were a sufficient number of fields of work, alongside that of the educated, theological apostolate, in which it was possible to put such a community into practice. These were all the fields in which, in the Christendom of that time, something like "Catholic Action" in today's sense of the word was desirable and necessary. For there was in fact no potential field of Christian activity that laymen in the state of the counsels did not make their own and cultivate at that period.

It was above all the Cistercians and the Teutonic Order who devoted their energy to agriculture, in particular the cultivation of the land and the colonization of vast areas, extending the Christian realm eastward; the dairy farms of the Cistercians were the model agricultural schools of the period, and other schools became affiliated with these. The history of art in all its branches, especially architecture, is not only indissolubly linked to the history of monasticism but is virtually identical with it;

[15] Pierre Felix Mandonnet, O.P., *Dante le théologien: Introduction à l'intelligence de la vie, des œuvres et de l'art de Dante Alighieri* (Paris: Desclée de Brouwer, 1935), 23f.

and every branch of artistic production lay in the hands of the monks. What the monks won for the kingdom of Christ in peaceful work, the spiritual knightly Orders conquered or defended with the sword. Bernard, who was so creative in the foundation and organization of the Templars, did not work fruitlessly in his aim to have the idea of chivalry in religious life emerge as a secular prolongation of the ideal of his own Order. The point was to integrate into the state of evangelical perfection all those areas of secular and natural activity that appeared to the classical ideal of the perfectly wise man, and even to the early Christian contemplative ideal, as something secondary or perhaps even something degrading; it was to prove that every honorable secular activity could be brought into unity with the state of evangelical perfection, to penetrate more and more forms of life with the ideal of perfection, to represent, without compromise, the life of Christ in these life forms; it was to provide the Christian people with the direct and irrefutable evidence that perfection is not alien to the world but is something possible and necessary everywhere. Thus, we see the Marian knights of the Teutonic Order founding and occupying whole provinces, engaging in commerce and organizing the means of transport, issuing coins and providing an ordered educational and legal system in their territories. Here, as in the other knightly Orders, a layman stood at their head as Grand Master, and the priests necessary for the pastoral care of the members within the Order were not privileged because of their office. The Order of Saint John, which was formed from a society for the service of the poor in Jerusalem into a knightly

Order, dedicated itself, in addition to its work in the care of the sick and the protection of roads for Crusaders and pilgrims, above all to the fight against Islam and piracy. Thus even the bloody business of war was given its place in the state of perfection, and even this branch of human activity was not only something that could take on some vague Christian meaning, but was a mission that could be united with the highest demands of Christian perfection. It was possible to take the solemn vows of poverty, chastity, and obedience and to combine these with the bearing of a sword, to bind them to the vows of defending the faith and serving the sick. It may be the case that the specific activity and the organization of the knightly Orders belonged to a particular time and that this is why they have not been able to maintain their place within the ecclesial organism (with the exception of the shadowy remains that have survived until the present day). Nevertheless, they remain a Christian experience and accomplishment of the highest significance, and the fundamental abandonment of this experience in later centuries could not mean anything but an impoverishment for the Church. The theological implications of this impoverishment have not yet been sufficiently understood, but they may at last become apparent in the coming age.

But the task of the lay Orders within Christendom was not only the establishment and the defense of the Christian soil and territory through peace and war, but every form of action born of Christian love. Already in the Middle Ages, the primary domains of the lay Orders were the two domains that have remained theirs until quite recently: the service of the sick and schools. Countless groups, some of them genuine Orders, some associations, some mere confraternities, devoted themselves to the service of the sick and, more recently, also to the service of the mentally ill (such as the Alexians and later on the Brothers of Saint John of God); in some Orders, such as the knightly Order of the Lazarites, a particularly striking image of the imitation of Christ, we see the care of the lepers embodied in such a way that both the sick and those who looked after them were together the members of one single Order. John of God, too, founded his Order as a layman for laymen, who were to distinguish themselves from people in the world only through their clothing and who took as a fourth vow the promise to care for the sick without payment for the whole of their lives. Each of their houses was to have one or two priests for pastoral work. When Pierre de Bethencourt's intellectual abilities did not suffice for the priesthood, he founded the Order of the Bethlehemites for the care of the sick and the instruction of the poor. More recently, the chimney sweep Peter Friedhofen formed the Society of the Merciful Brothers of Trier out of a youth group, for the care of the sick and other branches of charitable work.

The Trinitarians and Mercedarians provide an extreme example of living out Christian love in a manner stamped by religious life: they were founded for the liberation of Christians who had been captured as slaves, and they vowed not only to get hold of the money necessary to purchase the freedom of slaves, but if necessary to offer their own selves as a down payment for those who were to be ransomed. The number of those whom the

Trinitarians thus ransomed is estimated to be about 900,000. The Mercedarians, formed by Saint Peter Nolasco from an existing Catalan association of priests and knights, began as a spiritual knightly Order consisting of knights and brothers, who received their Augustinian-inspired constitution from Saint Raymond of Peñafort. Some of the brothers took Holy Orders. Later, because of rivalries between the Grand Council elected by the knights and the spiritual General elected by the brothers, and above all because of Pope John XXII's decision that a priest must always have the highest authority in the Order, the knights left, and the order henceforth became no longer a military Order, but only a religious one.

Alongside the brothers who care for the sick we find the brothers of the schools, who have expanded greatly in the modern period. Just as most founders established their communities almost by accident, so, too, did John de la Salle found the Brothers of the Christian Schools. Just as Benedict or Bruno or Francis or the seven Founders of the Servites had no notion, when they departed into solitude, that they were thus beginning the path toward a foundation; just as John of God did not intend to found an Order when he gathered a few laymen together to help him care for a hospital in Granada; so, too, de la Salle had no such plans when he rented a house for teachers whom he had persuaded to work in his free school in Rheims and shortly afterward gave them a common daily schedule. The outcome was a lay congregation whose members were not allowed to aspire to the priesthood; one who had already received major orders could not be accepted as a member. The scholasticates of such a congregation would naturally link their religious training with study at a higher institute or a university. Other teaching congregations, such as the Marianists, consist of priests, teaching brothers, and working brothers, all of whom have the same rights, even if their general superior, whose assistants are both priests and lay brothers, is always a priest! Countless lay associations from the Middle Ages up to the modern period, in the most diverse forms and areas of specialization, have all had the same goal: to instill in young people the ideal of a perfectly selfless life of service.

When we look at the Orders that emerged in the Middle Ages, what surprises us is not so much the number of those who entered the state of the counsels as the almost unlimited imagination of the Christian soul, which effortlessly devised ever new ways of embodying perfect love as Christ commanded it and living them out in a naively realistic form that was at one and the same time literal and sublimely heroic. Each group felt itself to be directly addressed by the gospel's demand to follow Christ perfectly, to sell everything, and to lay down one's life for the brethren. Each group was convinced that this highest ideal could be lived, not only by a few chosen ones who flee from the world, but by the group as such in a form appropriate to it. For example, someone asks: Would it not be the Lord's will to bring Christians who live far from one another closer together? And at once an Order, the Frères Pontifes, is formed of knights, priests, and ordinary workers, with the goal of building bridges—not only spiritual, ideal bridges, but utterly real bridges of stone, which can still be seen from Lyons to Avignon.

Ignatius of Loyola stands on the threshold between the Middle Ages and the modern period. He, too, was completely unclear about what God intended with him when he renounced his property and went into solitude, following the footprints of Francis and Dominic. He thought neither of priesthood nor of founding an Order. As a born knight, he sought the solution first of all in the imitation of the spiritual knightly Orders: he went to Jerusalem to spread the faith there and, if necessary, to defend it with weapons. External impossibility compelled him to take another path: it was a question of doing spiritually in the West what the knights of old had done physically in the East. So he began the path of studies: for a long time he thought, not of the priesthood, but of the tools he needed in order to proclaim the kingdom of God as a kind of itinerant preacher—for this is how he saw himself. He gathered a couple of disciples, laymen like himself, and he would have followed the plan he had at that time and sent them singly into the world to proclaim doctrine and give spiritual exercises as he himself wished to do if they had remained faithful to him. It was only conflicts with the Inquisition that opened his eyes more and more to the necessity of finishing his studies, that is, of becoming a priest, in order to be able to work as he had planned. Moreover, he saw that he had to form the companions who shared his vision into a more stable group if he was to give coherence to the movement that he wanted to start. Thus, the Society of Jesus became a priestly Order much more because of the world of education, which at that time was still organized in a medieval manner, than because of the intention of the founder. And when Ignatius later followed the traditional pattern in his Constitutions by directing to the priesthood those novices chosen for higher education, while he left the lay brothers without higher education and training, he followed much more the existing cultural situation here than his own personal wish. The time no longer existed, and had not yet arrived again, in which laymen could be given the specific tasks that belonged to the professed in the Society of Jesus; there was no reason, still less any possibility, to depart from the usual union of "clericus" and "priest" in the traditional sense. It was already audacious enough when Ignatius placed his apostles in the midst of the turmoil of the world without any monastery or prayer in choir. The significant mark of his personal disposition remains the fact that he expected indifference of every single one of the novices who entered with regard to whether or not they would study, whether they would become priests or remain laymen.[16] For him, the one thing necessary was the primary religious attitude of indifference, and priesthood and laity were, so to speak, a secondary matter contained within this indifference, which, once the divine vocation to the religious state had been grasped and accepted, awaited further specification from the mouth of the superior. Ignatius thereby said implicitly, in accordance with the original view of all the older Orders, that the primary vocation was not to the priesthood but to the imitation of Christ in the act of "leaving all things", whereas the determination to become a priest was a matter for the

[16] Ignatius Loyola, *Examen generale*, chap. 1, no. 11: "Omnes eadem animi dispositione (i.e., indifferentes quoad statum) ingredi oportet."

superiors in the Church or the Order. Recently, a Roman declaration has established the Church's relation to the priestly vocation in the same sense.[17]

If we survey the role of the priesthood within the state of the counsels from this vantage point, we see a certain development. First of all, priesthood was a function within the religious community. Then, when this community began to take on missionary activity and pastoral work, it became a kind of synthesis of the pastoral function (in the sense of today's secular clergy) and religious mission. Later still, through the influence of the medieval class structure, it became something bestowed as part of a universal education, and the member of the Order who needed this education to fulfill his tasks within the Order therefore became a priest. Since this link between the study of theology and the clerical career, which developed historically, has not been broken even into the most recent times, the Orders have accepted the existing situation without risking a change. The natural result of this for the laity has been an almost total lack of interest in creative theological work. They have occupied themselves with peripheral fields: Church history, exegesis, sociology, and also the comparative history of religion, the philosophy of religion, and metaphysics. For centuries they have not dared to broach central questions of dogmatics. This clericalization of theology has often been lamented, and with good reason, especially since theology has thus acquired a relatively strong practical and pastoral coloring. What lay

[17] Cf. *Acta Apostolicæ Sedis*, July 15, 1912. On this whole question: Lahitton, *Deux conceptions divergentes de la vocation sacerdotale* (1910). Brandenburger, "Vocatio sacerdotalis", *ZKT* (1914), 63–74.

people may be able to contribute to theology we have yet to see.[18] On the other hand, the Middle Ages also opened up for the first time a deep and tangible gulf between the

[18] It must nevertheless be recalled that the Church's theology was founded primarily by laymen. The apologists Justin, Tertullian, Clement, and Origen were laymen. The latter was ordained later against his will; he thereby initiates the long list of scholars and theologians who began as laymen and had to decide under pressure from others to accept the priestly office: Cyprian, Basil, Gregory Nazianzen, Jerome, Paulinus, Augustine, etc. Father B. Steidle, O.S.B., observes here: "It is obvious that the Church had a great interest in incorporating the teachers [of Christian theology] as closely as possible into the ecclesiastical organism through ordination to the priesthood" (*Die Kirchenväter* [Pustet, 1939], 60). The normal path of development of in fact the most important Fathers had three stages: first, study at a secular university; second, several years of monasticism (and hence of theological production); and, third, priestly ordination at the wish of the Church. With some variation, this was the path of Chrysostom (who was first a monk, but had to leave the monastery for reasons of health), of Athanasius, Basil, Gregory Nazianzen, Gregory of Nyssa, Jerome, Augustine, Gregory the Great, and others. This does not mean that their theology did not profit from their priesthood or, more precisely, from their practical involvement in the Church. All we wish to show is that the original path of the theologian went from the lay state via the religious state to the priestly state, so that theology originally lay in the hands of laymen and monks. We mention the names of only a few of those who remained laymen: Sextus Africanus, Pamphilus, Lactantius, Arnobius, Marius Victorinus, Prosper of Aquitaine. At most, one can say that the world view of patristic theology had a clear monastic coloring. For the Fathers, Christian perfection was basically identical with the realized state of the counsels. The whole theology of Alexandria, Cappadocia, and Africa bore the imprint of the counsels, and the monk-pope Gregory transmitted monastic theology to the Middle Ages. Only then did theology become "scholastic", i.e., an affair of the schools, and thereby primarily clerical, although of course the even later, modern identification of "clerical" with "priestly" (as we have shown) had not yet come about at that time.

secular clergy and the religious clergy, which in fact first allowed these states of life to come into being and confront one another consciously in their difference.[19] This is not the place to rehearse the vigorous controversies that arose through this differentiation, the reciprocal staking out of territories and, more significantly, of the ecclesial missions. What now concerns us is only that, from this point on, the priesthood became the "secular priest's" final goal, whereas for the religious priest who has renounced all self-determination, the priesthood can represent only an infinitely enriching gift of God that is mediated through his superior, and not something he has directly sought for its own sake. *Indifferentia* forbids him to seek and to receive the grace of the priesthood otherwise than in obedience, as an office and a function that he is given so that his monastic mission can be carried out more fully. If this mission demanded for some reason that he forgo this office—perhaps because it would be more of a hindrance than a help to his apostolic mission, or also because the superiors, without any explanation, did not bestow it on him—then he would have to accept this decision as the better situation, which would give greater glory to God. Examples of this are the school brothers who forgo the priesthood for the sake of their work or the brothers who care for the sick and, in order to be able to perform certain lowly services for them, prefer to forgo the priesthood, which they—rightly or wrongly

[19] Heitling, "Die professio der Kleriker und die Entstehung der drei Gelübde", *ZKT* 56 (1932); cf. idem, "Kanoniker, Augustinerregel und Augustinerorden", *ZKT* 54 (1930).

—do not believe to be very compatible with those services.[20] For the sake of the mission they have accepted in supernatural obedience, they forgo the graces and consolations that come from ordination.

The unprejudiced observer of the history of religious life is all the more astonished to see that there is no place today for the educated layman within the state of perfection. The de facto situation of the state of the counsels is still dominated by the historical and sociological laws of the Middle Ages and the Renaissance: the apostolate of the educated man today is possible only in the form of the clericate. If a student of medicine, of law, of the sciences or the arts, of engineering, or of architecture wants to realize the perfect imitation of Christ in his life today, no other path is open to him other than to abandon his job and study another discipline, namely, theology. The only reason justifying this demand comes from the development of history; it does not come from the gospel. What the gospel, which always has its purest expression at the time when Orders are founded, shows by contrast is that the state of perfection and the clericate by no means necessarily stand or fall together. It is only that the educated have not yet felt the pressing need to distinguish them. On the other hand, the form of the state of the counsels has not yet adapted itself to the new situation that has meanwhile arisen from the increasingly rapid differentiation and specialization of the branches of knowledge over the last few centuries.

We cannot conclude this historical assessment without

[20] Heimbucher, *Orden*, 1:607.

pointing out that all the great foundations of Orders sent waves of influence into the world of the laity. It would be surprising and suspicious were this not so, since the Orders, as "representatives" of the life of the gospel in the midst of history, exist in order to radiate their light into the whole Church, irrespective of whether their beams (according to the character of each Order) shine forth in a more contemplative or a more active way and thus provoke more contemplative or more active movements within the lay world. Concentric rings of tremors and ripples have thus always surrounded these center points where the lightning struck—or, to use another image, through the presence of a star the entire surrounding atmosphere is suffused with light. This phenomenon can be seen in the "Third" Orders, which have existed in every age to varying degrees of visibility and explicit organization and which then took on the somewhat different form of the "Marian congregation" in the case of the Jesuit Order. The essential point about these structures is that they are not primary, but secondary, an epiphenomenon that endures as long as the primary phenomenon does, as long as they are illuminated by their primary light source, but are doomed to perish when it goes out. An example of this is the fate of the "Marian congregation" after the abolition of the Society of Jesus. In some places ex-Jesuits, who held on to the previous structure to a certain extent, continued to look after it in the period of abolition, but otherwise it lost its original impetus and degenerated into a collection of pious confraternities. In their time of flourishing, both the Third Orders and the congregations achieved something indispensable; they enabled the spirit of an Order to bear fruit in the secular realm, and, ablaze with this spirit in the midst of the worldly state, they gave an example of a perfect Christian life through prayer, penitence, and the way they lived their life. They formed, as it were, the Order's arm and lever extended into the world and were thus to a large extent the precursors of "Catholic Action". At the same time, we must keep in mind in this context that the Third Orders, in their program and their rules, are only a kind of distant echo of the elemental event unleashed in the First and the Second Orders. Since they lack that act of "leaving all things" in a total following of Christ that constitutes the state of life and is the unity that gives form to all the deeds and practices making up the life of the counsels, the rules for tertiaries (unless these have been regulated at a subsequent stage) must necessarily fall apart into a certain multiplicity of regulations. We find this already in the original rule of the Franciscan tertiaries, which goes back to Francis of Assisi himself: "Besides prescriptions for practices of prayer and fasting, it demands simplicity in clothing, abstinence from dancing and theater, mutual help and especially the support of the poor and the sick, the payment of debts, the writing of one's will in good time, the reconciliation of disputes as well as refraining from bearing weapons and from unnecessary oaths."[21] It is more than evident that while all these prescriptions are excellent and have borne wholesome fruit in the course of the centuries, they presuppose rather than form a life-style; even less do they establish a form of life.

[21] Holzapfel, *Handbuch der Geschichte*, 661.

And the particular difficulty for all the regulated Third Orders has been how to find this style and this form[22] without drowning in a multiplicity of individual pious practices and prescriptions. It is significant here that the Franciscan Third Order was called into existence much more through the spontaneous enthusiasm of the laity than through any endeavor on the part of the First Order,[23] for indeed the Order initially put up a resistance when the guidance of the tertiaries was imposed on it as an obligation.[24] The influence of the Third Order can be explained not least by the fact that it carried out the first and most essential pioneer work in most places through its social and charitable activity. Since, over the course of time and especially in the nineteenth and twentieth centuries, this apostolate has been replaced by other kinds of associations, "it is clear that, for people in the world today, the Third Order must give up a great part of the activity it pursued earlier",[25] and thus it finds its chief goal in the personal deepening of religious life, in the "sanctification of oneself".

Something similar is true in the case of the Marian congregations of the Jesuits and for all the analogous groups of laity in the world that have been founded and nourished by more recent Orders. It is of course true that the congregations were originally intended to be much more apostolic than the Third Orders and that their remarkable

[22] Ibid., 679.
[23] Ibid., 669.
[24] Ibid., 662.
[25] Ibid., 671.

effectiveness in the old Society of Jesus[26] signified an unparalleled example of how the initial spirit of the Order can become contagious for those in the world. Nevertheless it is significant that the most immediate fruits were harvested among the youth who were taught in the Jesuit colleges, that is, at the age when the decision about one's state of life had not yet been taken and thus elements of both the religious and the worldly state could be combined in a sort of neutrality. At a later age, among the predominantly married people in the worldly state, the congregation could indeed promote a personal religious deepening through Marian piety, various prayers and consecrations, and charitable and apostolic works and could keep alive the Christian life of the layman, especially of the lay academic, but it goes without saying that the congregation could not blur the boundaries between the forms of the states of life by making the layman into a member of the Order: it could not take from him his worldly concerns and problems or communicate to him the simplicity and undividedness that grounds the state of the counsels as such. It is not surprising that even the great impetus of the congregations gradually ebbed away and had to yield to other structures, where they had previously been the sole masters of the field. Today it is above all youth groups who claim, just like the congregations, to transmit the formation of an elite and training in the apostolate, and this means that the congregations, and the Third Orders as well, are forced back onto the track

[26] Cf. Émile Villaret, S.J., *Les Congrégations Mariales*, vol. 1 (Paris: Beauchesne, 1947).

of inner "self-sanctification" without any corresponding external mission. The Catholic Action commentators explicitly shove them onto this track, along with the Third Orders and the confraternities who all form "auxiliary troops of Catholic Action", not its military kernel. We are not interested here in sorting out the questions about how these various bodies ought to be joined and interrelated. All that matters is the fact that the Catholic Action of the seventeenth and eighteenth centuries has yielded ground in many places to new Catholic Actions, which, however, are no longer the irradiation of an Order but are an organization belonging to the hierarchy. And thus the problem of the relation between the lay state and the state of the counsels is less resolved than ever.

3. The Demands of the Present Day

We can summarize the lesson of history in a single principle: The clericalization of the Orders has intensified in tandem with the increase in the secularization of the branches of education. This means that the state of the counsels has almost totally surrendered the positions in the world it held in the Middle Ages and has joined with the priestly state to form a block set off against the lay state in the world. Within the Orders that exist today, with the exception of certain school congregations, there is no longer any place for an educated layman. In these Orders, the layman now occupies only the subordinate posts that facilitate life in the monastery and in the Order for the educated clerical monk: domestic service, the kitchen, agriculture, carpentry, and technical work, perhaps at best printing and secretarial work. The subordinate position given to the lay brothers is clearly one factor in the serious vocational problems that very many Orders have today, although this difficulty has more to do with the general social problems of our age than with specific questions of how the Orders are organized. The point we are making here is that it is practically impossible today to lead the life of the evangelical counsels as a doctor, lawyer, politician, journalist, and so on, in secular positions, since only the theologian is permitted to combine the life of the counsels with a professional course of study. The first effect of this is an apathy, which is difficult to put one's finger on but undeniably present, on the part of the educated laity not only vis-à-vis the state of the counsels, but also vis-à-vis the pronouncements that the hierarchy make about the professional fields of the laity. In order to reduce this gap, many a theologian from the secular and the religious clergy has been sent to do special professional studies after finishing his theology, so that he would have the competence and the right to make a contribution regarding the "borderline questions" that the laity face; but the layman will remain uncomfortable and will have a perhaps unspoken objection to this competence on the part of the theologians, as long as the latter have not come to know the lay profession from within, as it is concretely lived and practiced. All reassuring and conciliatory opinions aside, one would not be wrong to make the claim that the great majority of Catholic doctors in practice take little or no notice of the Roman regulations and pronouncements that affect them; that, in difficult borderline cases, many of the best of them hold personal conscience as the ultimate authority for a decision; and that many, when faced with the specific choice of a profession (here the author speaks from experience) refrain from choosing the specialty of gynecologist, for example, only because, in the present state of affairs, they do not want to land in what they call insoluble difficulties. This unhappy situation, which has its parallels in other professions, is surely due at least in part to the distrust that the Catholic specialist ultimately harbors—perhaps wrongly—against all the regulations that a nonspecialist makes for him. Even if one were to explain to him that, standing behind these pronouncements are not only theologians who have not studied the special professional questions, but also genuine specialists who have been asked for their opinion and consulted in a thorough manner: even then, as things are today, a basic distrust would linger. The gap between the specialized professional and his praxis, on the one side, and the specialized theologian in the diocesan or religious clergy, on the other, has become too great to permit a calm discussion of professional questions. And it is precisely because the lawyer or politician feels so incompetent in ultimate theological questions that he cannot concede to the theologian an ultimate competence in the secular professional field. But even today it is possible to find a platform on which the priest and the layman could encounter one another as equals, not standing over against one another from the outset as the "teaching" Church and the "listening" Church, but with equal rights stemming from the same ultimate responsibility and mission: namely, the state of the counsels. Here, not only would the theologian speak to the layman on the same level, but, even more importantly, the layman himself would learn how to assess the secular situation on the basis of the full experience of the "state of perfection". Every feeling of inferiority, no matter how unconscious, that so often handicaps even the best of the laity in the world when they must make lonely Christian decisions would fall away, and the judgment of the layman within his area of specialization would necessarily carry the same weight within the Church as the professional theologian's judgment, where the latter is not explicitly the bearer of ecclesial office.

But all this is only an external and negative consideration. The decisive and positive element here is that when the secular sphere is reconquered for the spiritual state of life, the entire blessing, the entire grace, that lies within the total immolation of the vows will necessarily flow into the secular professional jobs: the grace of the renunciation itself—of one's own possessions, of family, and of self-determination—would flow over onto every patient, client, employee, and worker with whom the consecrated layman had dealings. Then there is the grace of contemplation, without which a life in the state of the counsels is unthinkable and which must be made accessible regardless of circumstances to the layman who lives in the state of the counsels. The defect of "Catholic Action" that we discovered at the outset—namely, that it does not find its point of rest and its nurturing substance in a Catholic contemplation cultivated in accordance with its mission—would fall away. The time that the married layman must dedicate to his family or to the acquisition and administration of his goods becomes free time and can be used for God, for prayer, penance, and contemplation. The leisure for reflection, solitude, and reading, which the layman so sorely misses because of the stress of his profession, would certainly be available, more richly available indeed, than to a diocesan priest consumed by parish work, because the layman is usually better able to set the boundaries of his own activity. This seems to allow us to square the circle and actually resolve the essential problem of the lay apostolate, which is usually held to be insoluble: the harmonious and tranquil unity of action and contemplation. Thanks to this unity, the layman would never need to fear being unfaithful to his spiritual mission even in the most worldly turmoil of his professional work. For he would not have chosen this mission for himself; it would have been entrusted to him in the obedience of the counsels, and he would carry out under obedience all that it entails, even what appeared its most worldly dimension. In Christian terms, his work would be just as fruitful as any activity carried out in monasteries. By virtue of the total revaluation that the most neutral deeds receive through obedience, the entire blessing belonging to the renunciation would pour forth—surely for the first time in the history of the Church—over all areas of Christian activity.

It is scarcely possible to gauge a priori the springs of supernatural power that would be unleashed in such a life. Working in the same practice, office, or factory, but freed from the absorbing and often depressing concerns about family and earnings, the layman in the state of the counsels would have an incomparable advantage in terms of time, freedom, and productivity, not to mention the possibilities of taking up deeper questions that may not be immediately lucrative but are much more necessary, when seen with Christian eyes: public questions for which those with such busy private lives have no time, questions affecting the Church in the civil sphere, in which married people, who are dependent in so many ways, perhaps do not want to take the risk of getting their fingers burned, questions of the apostolate in the lay milieu, which the priest finds it impossible or at least difficult to approach. Youth groups can exhibit something of this advantage vis-à-vis the associations of married men, which always display a much slower tempo in comparison. And yet not even the youth groups offer all the possibilities that could be offered by a community of lay people dedicated to God in the world. For here the main point would not be the formation of the members but the mature involvement of those who had been formed. Prayer, contemplation, the spirit of penitence, and the readiness for total involvement would already be presupposed from the outset. And the secular institute would be inspired by a personal spirit, a spirituality that is proper to the state of the counsels, and to it alone, within the Church.

But not only this. If what is involved in today's "Catholic Action" is the reconquering for the Church of the positions that have been lost in the world, and if this is possible only through the apostolate from layman to layman, from colleague to colleague,[1] then this is possible with full effectiveness only when these apostles present

[1] "In order to lead back to Christ . . . such wide circles of society, a selection from their midst of well-trained lay helpers is required, who are intimately acquainted with their entire mode of thought and their

to the eyes of their colleagues, not a mere approximation to the perfect Christian,[2] but rather the greatest measure of such perfection that can be attained among human beings and sinners. But this fullest measure already exists within the framework of the "state of perfection", the state of the counsels.[3] It is important to allow Christians today to understand that the one who chooses the vowed form of life does not turn his back on the "world" and become an eccentric foreign to the present age, still less an egotistic specialist in his own perfection, but rather is one who does nothing other than strip away all that is his own, all that holds him back, so that he can be totally free for the will of God, the path of Christ, the mission of the Church. The personal renunciation that lies in following the three counsels, and that embraces in principle everything that belongs to a man—possessions, body, and soul—is not an end in itself; still less is perfection an end in

---

interests and who find the path to their hearts in an attitude of brotherly friendship. The first and nearest apostles among the workers must be workers, and the apostles of the world of industry and of commerce must likewise come from this world": Pius XI, *Quadragesimo anno*.

[2] In German: "den vollkommenen Christen". A note by the editor states that the author explained this term elsewhere as "den voll gekommenen Christen", "the Christian who has fully arrived"—TRANS.

[3] L. v. Hertling, *Theologia ascetica* (Rome: Universitas Gregoriana, 1944): "Summa adeoque vera et unica perfectio proponitur ab Ecclesia in statu perfectionis (24). Ideo etiam pro iis, qui non sunt de statu religiosorum, vita religiosa norma et exemplar perfectionis christianæ esse potest et debet" (37): "The Church proposes the religious state as the highest, true, and sole perfection" (24). "Therefore the religious life can and must be the norm and exemplar of Christian perfection even for those who do not belong to the religious state" (37).

itself; it is the presupposition and the basis for making the whole of one's life a pure expression of the life of Christ. Only the one who "leaves everything" can in this literal sense choose and receive, in the place of the contents of his life, the command by which the Lord sends him out, as the meaning of his life. Since the Orders (and communities like them) have always been the nurseries of holiness, there is today no more direct way to bear holiness into the spheres and the professional jobs of the laity than this combination of the lay state with the state of the counsels. This is not only the way to broaden the field of holiness as such, but no less importantly in concrete terms, it is the way to establish the pure Christian type of professional work for the most diverse lay professions: when it has been displayed in life, it can then be reflectively and theoretically understood and recorded. The specialized movements of "Catholic Action" have indeed been concerned for a long time with this pure type and with the particular, often very difficult questions of the professional ethos of the various branches. But little that is comprehensive has emerged in this area, mainly because the professionals who are genuinely involved in praxis no longer have the time for such work. No one would be better suited to deal theoretically with the questions of professional ethos than one who lived these questions in praxis and also had the leisure to spare for reflecting on them.

We must draw attention to yet another special type of man and professional work, a type that often lives in a kind of remarkable oscillating midpoint between turning to the world and asceticism, between the secular state and the state of the counsels: namely, the artist. Often enough, because of his professional work and the demands it makes, he stands naturally in the position where a layman in the life of the counsels would stand supernaturally. Out of a profound inner distance to the world and to the things of the world, he must nevertheless create in the greatest proximity to them, in a continual struggle with them; more than anyone else, he has a mission and an awareness of mission that bring him into an almost uncanny closeness to the priest and the religious. And if he is, moreover a Christian artist, if, like the architect of a medieval cathedral, he is compelled to draw his art out of the most intimate mysteries of the knowledge of God, then the two forms of mission draw even closer to one another, even if they never completely coincide. There remains a gulf: the pure religious receives his mission in total *indifferentia* from God through the superior. The artist, obsessed by his mission, already bears this mission in himself, and no one can bestow it on him from the outside or take it from him. And yet there can be cases —isolated, but extremely significant—in which a natural and a supernatural mission come together to form a unity. It is at least worth reflecting on the fact that Dante belonged to the clerical state, that Calderón became a priest after having been a soldier, that Claudel struggled for years with the question of a religious vocation and was sent back into the world only after an unsuccessful attempt in a Benedictine monastery, that so many artists have remained unmarried, that we find profound tragedy in so many marriages of Catholic artists in the modern period, casting its shadows over their whole œuvre (certainly without any benefit to their literary work and their religious mission). It is merely superficial to object that an artist has to have experienced, enjoyed, and learned more of the world than is compatible with the state of the counsels. Sin can never be one of the presuppositions for carrying out a Christian mission, and sin itself never has any constructive, creative power. Christian knowledge of the world, as Christ himself, his immaculate Mother, and his saints possessed it, is no partial knowledge that needs to be filled out by another knowledge: it is the true, complete knowledge, and not only does it suffice for every artistic creation, but it is in fact the only thing needed. The state of perfection could become the framework in which the creative man, even the genius, would find his highest development as God desires it. What would Pascal have become if he had encountered a community that really suited him instead of the pseudo-monastery of the Jansenists; or Schiller, who through a profound affinity had such a good understanding of the ideal of the Maltese Order; or Baudelaire, if he had only opened himself wholly to the unconditional, divine demands in his soul—to say nothing of Kierkegaard, who (as Erik Peterson has shown) lacked only the monastic form of life, which would have allowed him to fulfill his specific supramatrimonial mission, not in an unchristian melancholy, but in a Christian community.

Any of these paths offer the possibility of an encounter between total secular competence and total Christian competence. If such encounters were to come about, the word "layman" would lose its connotation of "dilettante" or "non-specialist". As long as the clergy and religious together represent "religious specialists", the layman in the ecclesiological sense will also feel himself to be a "layman" in the secular-natural sense of the word. He will leave this position only when, standing on the ground of the state of the counsels, he ranks as a "specialist" along with the diocesan and religious priest, sharing equal rights, perhaps not in the professional questions of theology, but nonetheless in questions of the life of the spirit, of prayer, and of perfection. Thus he will become the true "hyphen" that "Catholic Action" seeks between the secular profession and the official Church. His obedience will enable him to be an "executive organ", without thereby abandoning his professional independence and responsibility. The required "formation" of the intellect and will of the one who carries out the task by the intellect and will of the one who commands does in fact presuppose the relationship of the counsel of obedience. If the renunciation of the right to determine one's own life were not carried out wholly on the religious level, in a true and fully conscious sacrifice in the imitation of Christ, then a relationship of total obedience would always threaten to oscillate between worldliness and spiritual manipulation. If obedience became the form of such a community, the result would be a feverish group of military shock-troops —never the free and peaceful force of men who have personally consecrated their whole life to Christ and who thus, in a manner that the world cannot understand, share in the mystery of Christ's free obedience to the Father.

4. *Concrete Forms*

If at this point we raise certain questions concerning concrete forms, it is not in the least with the intention of giving guidelines and rules to any communities that now exist or that will be called forth in the future. Communities of this sort are not founded on paper but in the life of those appointed by God. Instead, we are here concerned with the most general characteristics, such as they follow from what we have been saying, things that would characterize every undertaking of this kind a priori and with a certain necessity. And we are not groping in the dark here, for the Constitution *Provida Mater* in fact already provides the indications necessary for shaping these communities, broad enough to be adapted by associations of every kind for their own specific goal, but also clear enough that they retain a distinctive face and a commonality.

Article 3, number 2, of *Provida Mater* speaks of the inner presuppositions for "the recognition of a pious association of believers as a secular institute", and first of all of the "consecration of the life" of those who "vigorously strive for the perfection of the Christian life in a special manner, beyond those practices of piety and renunciation to which all who aim at this perfection must commit themselves . . . through the profession of celibacy and perfect chastity made before God, which must be confirmed through vows, an oath, or a consecration binding in conscience, according to the constitutions; through the oath or promise of obedience", through which they "in all respects always stand inwardly under the hand and guidance of the superiors"; "through vows or promises of poverty, by virtue of which they cannot use earthly goods freely, but only in a circumscribed and limited way as set forth in the constitutions".

The three vows, which are the unshakable foundation of the life of the counsels, are not watered down for the layman who enters the state of the counsels but are adapted to his proper conditions of life. This adaptation can entail difficult concrete problems, but it is not in the least to be understood as a fundamental compromise with the "world" or as something that can be carried out in practice only through such a compromise. The counsels take their measure and their ideal, not from forms that have grown up in the course of history, but from the gospel and from the Lord's intention when he called his disciples to follow him in a total renunciation.

No fundamental questions ought to arise regarding *chastity*. It is clear and indivisible in a way that no other counsel is. Practical and pastoral problems of a new kind arise only where a layman must live among laymen, without enclosure and religious habit. These problems are not insoluble, but what they therefore demand is a stricter selection of novices than in the Orders with enclosure and habit, as well as a healthy, strong, and positively ordered asceticism that, in the power of the deeper and stronger unity of love between Christ and the Church, can look utterly unabashedly at questions about sexuality, love, and marriage, and not negatively or prudishly hush them up. Why indeed could one not imagine a Christian virginal doctor who draws the force for chastity from his vow and does not let himself be confused by any demonstration or examination? Is not the same demand made of every Catholic student of medicine before his marriage, at a period in his life when chastity is perhaps essentially harder than it is later in his praxis? And have not experienced congregations of brothers with the vow of chastity carry out all ministrations to (male) patients, including the setting of catheters, without, as those with experience put it, encountering any difficulties worth mentioning? To the contrary, should we not be surprised at the scrupulousness of many female congregations, who are not themselves permitted to carry out important services for their patients and employ secular lay people for these tasks—who even maintain birth clinics, although their rule does not allow them to be present at a birth, even in an auxiliary capacity? There is no doubt that the nineteenth century opened the doors to a hypersensitivity and a prim prudishness in questions of chastity that was completely unknown in the baroque period, still less in the Middle Ages, and this attitude often seems to gain ground in ecclesiastical circles today the more the "world" finds its way back to the earlier candor in sport and the physical culture. Perfect chastity in the world, especially for men, can be achieved only on the basis of an attitude that has reflected on and come to grips with all the questions of the body, of sexuality, and of love: on the basis of the knowledge of how much all that is bodily belongs in Christ to the "*sacramentum magnum* of Christ and the Church" and how much virginity signifies a superabundant fulfillment of all the fruitfulness of human love. But perhaps the decisive difficulties do not lie so much in the realm of sexual continence as in that of intellectual loneliness and the need for complementary relationships, so that a lay Order can be conceived only in terms of a strong community that bears, fulfills, and nourishes the individual member.

It is *obedience* that will pose the hardest problems in a community that has its life in secular spheres, jobs, and obligations. The members must be allowed truly to root themselves in their job, with the social obligations that doing so entails, for there is no other way of carrying out their work fruitfully; but, on the other hand, there can be no question of giving them full freedom over their undertakings and decisions and making only a sphere of their inner life, which is cleanly separate from the secular-professional sphere, accessible to the oversight and guidance of the superior. Such a dualism would make obedience in the sense of the state of the counsels, obedience as an "immolation", impossible. This is why other paths must be found in such institutes to make the entire secular activity of a member dependent on supernatural obedience, beginning from the choice of profession (if the one who enters does not already have one) and covering the course of studies, the taking up of a practice or position, as well as the positive or negative response to nominations, appointments, promotions, and changes. Given the contemporary work situation, it should not be difficult to enter into contracts only for a limited time, or in any case so that it is possible for the superior to transfer a member without much difficulty. The community member must maintain a fundamental, deeply rooted *indifferentia* concerning his profession at the beginning of his working career and throughout the course of it, and the superior will occasionally make use of his right, in love, to prevent the assumption from gaining ground that a member installed in his practice cannot be touched. The member must also be ready, like every member of an established Order or religious community, to take another job, to abandon a work that may perhaps be flourishing, or to accept a form of activity that he does not like or for which he feels perhaps unsuited or insufficiently prepared, if the superior so wishes it. An obedience that could not touch and move the basis of one's whole existence would not be obedience in keeping with the evangelical counsel. To make concessions here would be to strike at the very essence of the state of the counsels; the result would be at best a hybrid structure without clarity or consistency, a misbegotten creature that would prove incapable of life. On the other hand, rootedness in the secular discipline must be taken seriously, so seriously that one must take special provisions against ill-considered and imprudent arbitrariness on the part of a superior: for example, a committee formed of professional colleagues of the member in question—remotely like the delegations of the seven "tongues" in the Maltese Order—so that the major superior could have permanent representatives and counselors from each professional group. Despite these safeguards, obedience must be applied all the more strictly, the greater the danger that one may use secular ties and obligations to escape from it.

Poverty will be perfect in terms of the spirit, but the manner of living it must be in keeping with one's circumstances. The perfection will consist in the attitude of utter dependence in the disposition of things and in the impossibility of possessing or acquiring anything for oneself, rather than in a demonstrative lack of that which is necessary for a life in keeping with one's state. This dependence will be more embarrassing and humiliating for one who lives in the world than for the monk in his monastery, where asking for permission is often more of a ceremony than an inner humbling. It will indeed not be possible for a very busy professional man in the world to ask the superior for permission in every trifling matter. He will be given a certain measure of freedom in the disposition of money, time, and the way he lives his life, but he must give all the stricter account of this administration. The example of Paul the tentmaker can show that this form of poverty is no less perfect than the form that connects lack of possessions with lack of earnings: Paul finds it more perfect to link his apostolate with a secular job than to be a burden on the communities—as other apostles do and as he, too, could permit himself to do. A lay institute could learn much from this union of a secular job with the greatest apostolic generosity. Paul also insists that *everyone* should earn money, simply in order to be able to exercise the Christian duty of almsgiving. Accordingly, the directive of the Gospel: "You received without paying, give without pay" (Mt 10:8) refers more to the supernatural goods that the priest, first of all, but also the charismatic and the one who lives in the state of the counsels has received and for which he ought not to accept any payment.

Provida Mater goes on to speak of the incorporation of members and of the obligation this entails. The bond that unites the members with the institute must be "firm": either for life or for a limited time, after which it must be renewed. "The bond . . . must be reciprocal and complete, so that the one who enters gives himself wholly to the community in accordance with the constitutions, and the community cares for the member and supports him." Regarding foundations and houses, it states: "Although the secular institutes do not require their members to live in common or under a single roof", they must "nevertheless, for the sake of emergencies, and out of considerations of usefulness, have one or more houses in common, in which (1) the regional or, in particular, the general directors can live; (2) aspirants can live or meet, in order to receive or further their formation, to make retreats, and for other similar purposes; (3) it is possible to house those members who because of sickness or other circumstances cannot look after themselves, or for whom it is not good to live alone or in others' households."

This outline of the external framework raises a number of weighty questions. First, regarding community: Every Order is a community and must display this community visibly and tangibly. The Christian is not a loner who lives lost somewhere in the Church: Christ himself founded a community, a kind of supernatural family, and the Church has continually encouraged endeavors to live in common, gathering together the hermits who did not themselves join to form a cenobium and breaking the strict silence of the Carthusians. It would be impossible, it would run contrary to the mind of the Church, to send out today's apostles like hermits into the wilderness of the world, the big city, the factories. Rather, even the most solitary and exposed apostolate that contemporary circumstances might demand ought to be risked only with the support of a strong community. This is the only way to overcome the danger of the apostle becoming alienated from the community, losing himself in the relations, families, and friendships of his milieu, and finally becoming lost to the community altogether. *Quadragesimo anno*, too, demands this close association of the laity for effective action, and Cardinal Suhard emphasized this in a particular way in his 1947 pastoral letter: "The guarantee for the inner life of the apostles and for their moral perseverance and their mutual strengthening lies in the community. This does not necessarily mean living together physically. It presupposes above all a spirit of community. It demands that the messengers of the good news not act like renegades but rather dedicate themselves to a single action in the total consensus of their points of view and methods. This will produce a tenfold result."[1] Experience and the favorable and unfavorable circumstances of the future will teach what external form this community may take—whether it is expressed in frequent central meetings or more in regional contacts or whether it perhaps cannot be realized for long periods except in small or very small groups living together in one place, or indeed perhaps in local meetings, where it is impossible or infeasible to live together. Where a spirit of the counsels lives, such questions can always be resolved.

More difficult is surely the question of which profes-

[1] *Die Entscheidungsstunde der Kirche*, trans. Hans Urs von Balthasar, *Christ heute* 1/1 (Einsiedeln: Johannes Verlag, 1947), 63.

sional occupations can be brought together in such an institute. It is no longer possible in the secular and social sphere to have the sharp separation between educated and uneducated that led in the Middle Ages to the distinction between choir monks and lay brothers and, in the Society of Jesus, to that between priests and lay brothers. Countless types of educational institutions and levels of degree programs lead in an almost unbroken chain from the university lecturer to the simple office employee and worker, so much so that even the third category that the Society of Jesus inserted between professed and lay brothers, the "educated coadjutors", who in the founder's view should be priests with a less complete education than the professed, is scarcely an adequate response to the plurality that exists today. Higher and lower classes in the medieval Orders, in the monastic and knightly Orders and in the Third Orders had no problems in living together in fraternity, because, on the one hand, a new hierarchy entered the scene in the monastic Orders, and, on the other hand, the distinctions between social classes were not blurred in the knightly Orders and were even more preserved in the Third Orders. In a modern community one will have to reflect with great care on what forms and stages of education and the lack of education can come together to form a genuine and lasting community and what tensions would be too great to risk in the long term. Since, however, such a community in any case will be suitable only for a few and will require special qualities of spirit and of character, the selection itself will bring together similar types of people. Nevertheless, the question will remain, and one will either proceed to establish various levels within the same community or to group together members with a similar educational status in different institutes—unless the chaotic times that seem to be fast approaching shake up the social ranks in society so thoroughly that, at least for a period, people of all classes could, in the state of the counsels, meet each other on one level: as a human being, a Christian, a consecrated person.

But the idea of the new religious knight could stand as a contrast to the desolation and meaninglessness of the impending society of ant-men, reduced to the same level and indistinguishable from each other, this nightmare that weighs ever more heavily on those Christians who still understand what social degree, rank, and inner dignity mean; this idea could represent the last effective bulwark against such a danger, like Rhodes and Malta against the Turks. Unlike the religious knight of an earlier age, he would not make an outward show of his noble view of the world; in the midst of a world of proletarian uniformity, he would embody the indestructibility of inner nobility, and he would do so on all levels of society, in every job and milieu. He would also be free, without becoming a fruitless historicist, to possess the good things of the past in a living way and to hand these on in an age in which perhaps no one else would have the leisure to burden himself with the useless and superfluous dimension of the spirit. Where natural society abandoned rank and nobility, he would preserve their imperishability because of his rootedness in the supernatural.

If this idea takes hold, the candidates would be only too numerous; the prospect of a life without concern for one's daily bread and, even more, the prospect of an enticing "synthesis" between the advantages of religious life and life in the world would tempt many—and thus the selection would have to be made all the more rigorously. For the task is difficult, indeed very difficult, if the entire institute is not to succumb in a short time to the dangers of secularization. A hard novitiate with iron consistency, in total seclusion, would have to precede the higher studies, which would be best pursued in some kind of college. Here the students would follow their individual courses of study, but they would have the opportunity in the house for further education in a philosophy and theology adapted to their specialization as well as for an introduction to all the questions of their eventual life in the counsels. The period of testing before being admitted definitively would be very long and would include not only the time of education, but also a sufficient period in which they would have to prove themselves in their practical profession. The members would have frequent contact with each other and with the superior, and they would be required to come together often for spiritual renewal and times of recollection, prayer, contemplation, and deep reflection on Holy Scripture. Other meetings would bring together members who have the same specialization to discuss common questions affecting their world view and their professional work.

In conclusion, there are two questions we have to address: the question of the visibility of such an institute and that of its attitude toward the priesthood. The first question would become relevant as soon as the institute was founded; the second perhaps only much later.

Timid spirits, disturbed by the perspectives opened up here and concerned above all that the members should have the best possibilities for their work, will advise against visibility. It will be said that such lay people would be "marked men" who would not be given the more important jobs; not only unbelievers but even Catholics and professional colleagues would avoid them and would view this new and unusual kind of Christian with suspicion. This objection is understandable. Would it not be better to allow such men, who want to dedicate themselves totally to God's cause in their professional work, to bind themselves individually through private vows and at most to exert their influence in a loose fellowship without any further organization, in a kind of circle of friends (like the George Circle, for example)? Did not Peter Lippert see the future development of the state of the counsels in this direction, in his "Letters in a Monastery"? And do not many signs of the times, such as the youth movement, point to this? The answer is that such "associations" are certainly possible in the future but that they can never be the basis of what we call the state of the counsels. The state of the counsels entails a firm obedience, not only personal guidance, not only a relationship between master and disciple. But such an obedience is possible in the long term only in a stable community whose structure is not subject to the vacillations of personal whims. The strongly emphasized objectivity of the rule and the structure is a necessary characteristic of the form of life of the counsels. But such a structure cannot be invisible: first, for practical reasons, because the common religious and academic training of a large number of gifted people cannot remain hidden; but, more importantly, for theoretical reasons, too, because the Catholic Church is a visible Church with visible states of life that are established through visible sacraments and consecrations. Thus, it can be correct to hide one's own state of life in periods of immediate danger for the Church—for example, during the French Revolution—and in other exceptional situations, such as when making one's vows known would lead to conflict in one's immediate surroundings or to direct disadvantages for the Church. But a state of life in the Church is per se something visible: living secretly in the state of the counsels ought to be considered just as much an exception as a secret marriage, and this is how it was looked on in earlier, Catholic times. Experience shows that people are more suspicious of lay groups that they think may be living the evangelical counsels than of those that are publicly open about their state. In one of Italy's big cities, a priest united the protagonists and leaders of "Catholic Action" to form a kind of secret lay Order with vows: the effect was a widespread uneasiness in the area. Every sensible person had to wonder whether these unmarried men were religious or not, and what law of life, what directives they followed. The Little Brothers and Sisters of Father Charles de Foucauld had the opposite effect; they appeared in the factories and among the communist workers in their religious habit, which consisted of the poorest working clothes with the Cross sewn on the side, and after initial surprise and brief resistance, they conquered their hearts. "So have no fear of them; for nothing is covered that will not be revealed, or hidden that will not be known. What I tell you in the dark, utter in the light; and what you hear whispered, proclaim upon the housetops" (Mt 10:26–27). The states of life in the Catholic Church are visible. They can be made invisible only as a result of the blurring of distinctions between the states of life or the fading of an awareness of the states of life, and these ghosts haunt us, too, thanks to secularization and to Protestantism. This does not mean that the member of a lay community must explain the essence and the form of his institute to everyone without discrimination. It simply means that the institution as such is not disguised and that the apostle of Christ confesses openly for whose sake he bears the fetters of celibacy, of poverty, and of obedience.

Nor can the second question be avoided: the attitude the lay Order adopts toward the priesthood. Without anticipating how things may develop in the future and what solutions may perhaps be attempted, we ought nevertheless to look into what may be a distant future and try to sketch the idea of a synthesis between the lay state in the sense of profession and the priesthood in the sense of office. Indeed, in light of the medieval synthesis between *clericus* and *sacerdos*, this idea is not so far-fetched as it may initially appear; it would be nothing but the Church's endeavor to prevent the specializations of the sciences and professions from becoming a process of secularization in the sense of an alienation from the ministerial office. One must of course at once recall the difference we mentioned above between priestly ordination for the secular priest and that for the religious priest. Whereas the secular priest is primarily the pastor of a specific, delimited flock, to whom he mediates the Word of God and the sacraments, the religious priest is primarily an apostle who scatters the seed of God in the world across all the boundaries of parishes and dioceses—though it is indeed possible that he be put for a time at the disposal of a bishop for parochial ministry. Paul thanks God that he did not baptize anyone in Corinth, "for Christ did not send me to baptize but to preach the gospel" (1 Cor 1:14–17). When the layman in the state of the counsels is given priestly functions, it is to perfect his apostolic function (in action and in contemplation); he makes use of them only insofar as they serve the needs of his apostolate. It follows that one must say: a lawyer, a doctor, a journalist, and so on, who is the member of a secular institute would be ordained priest whenever it served the needs of his Christian apostolate. It does not lie beyond the realm of possibility that the Church might one day willingly consider this idea, which seems fantastic today, in the midst of the political and religious upheavals toward which the hollow hull of Europe seems to be heading. If all regular pastoral care organized in the traditional way had become impossible, or at least subject to innumerable hindrances, how many believers would rejoice that they could receive the sacraments and the Word of God from men who externally carried out a lay profession but were equipped with the faculties of ordination? And who would be more appropriate for this than a layman consecrated to God? Furthermore, and perhaps closer to us: what if—instead of the nonsense laid upon souls in psychology, pathology, and psychoanalysis, a pseudoscience that is often nothing more than a truly satanic caricature of sacramental confession—a Catholic doctor who had a thoroughly Christian understanding, founded on the Gospels, of the art of healing souls also had the power to hear their confession in the name of Christ and to impart his absolution? Or what if a lawyer possessed such authority that he could reconcile people not only with one another but with God? One could also ask whether the heroic experiments of "Catholic Action" in France, where educated and ordained clerics go into the factories to renew a direct contact with the workers, might not in time find better success by following the opposite path: what if, instead of making the clerics workers, one were to bestow the functions of a priest on the workers who were suited to it? This would solve at one stroke the thorny question of adapting to the workers' milieu, since the worker priest himself would be drawn immediately from the working class. This would of course presuppose that such a priest were given the training that precisely corresponded to his class and the education of his milieu. Such an adaptation—not of theology as a science, but of the priestly formation, to the future milieu in which the apostle must work—is not in the least a utopian ideal, and a deliberate and magnanimous start has already been made in France and in other countries. Certain isolated cases are surely very provocative, such as the priest of a Roman working-class area who was once a chauffeur. After a quick, personal introduction into the field of work from the bishop and without ever having set foot in a seminary, he was ordained and installed as parish priest, where he achieves astonishing success among the workers today. These are admittedly individual cases, but they are not infrequently indications of future possibilities for the Church. Finally, more for the sake of completeness and without for the moment any prospect of putting the idea into practice, one can ask what kind of pastoral training a doctor or technician ought to receive, if he were a member of a secular institute and were to receive priestly ordination.[2] Naturally, one must not overlook other experiences in recent years, such as the almost universal observation that when workers recognize one of their colleagues to be a priest and have confidence in him as their

[2] A great deal has been said in recent years about lay theology. On the basis of the questions we are raising, we must distinguish between three possible senses: (1) Lay theology can first of all denote a theology tailored for laymen, i.e., those who are not professional theologians; it would thus represent a popularized, "universally comprehensible" presentation of exact research in relation to the professional form of this research. Most of the "lay dogmatic treatises" are written by professional theologians, and it is easy to understand that professional circles have little interest in these texts. (2) The word is used in a completely different sense when it refers to a theology written by laymen who were not clerics but were trained theologians; thus, many of the Fathers were active as theologians before receiving priestly ordination. Such a theology would deserve to be taken with full seriousness in a professional context, but it would probably lack some specifically clerical traits, e.g., a strongly pastoral orientation in the selection and treatment of the themes. (3) A third form would be a theology (written either by priests or laymen) addressed to laymen in the state of the counsels, who require a solid theological education for their total apostolate in addition to a different kind of professional training. Such a theology would have to meet two basic demands: concentration on the essential matter of revelation and its interpretation, on dogmatics (here, the "clerical" branches such as pastoral theology, moral theology, canon law, homiletics, etc., could move more into the background, depending on the lay professional work of each student); and on the orientation of the material to the needs of the specifically lay apostolate.

friend, they do not want him to continue as a manual worker: not because of tradition, but through a spontaneous feeling that they want him to dedicate himself totally to his spiritual tasks and to be the father of their newly founded community. Many different experiences must be collected here and their relative significance assessed. The suburban parishes of Paris—to mention only these—with their movement reminiscent of the early Christians and their charismatic fervor, have loosened up structures that seemed utterly rigid and have realized things that looked impossible, but, on the other hand, they have raised so many open questions that it is not yet possible to speak the last word on this subject.

But the layman in the state of the counsels must always be indifferent about the priesthood, since he would receive it, not for his personal consolation, but as an instrument of his mission. Thus he would receive it where it would be beneficial to his special mission, but he would forgo it—even if this renunciation were difficult for him—where it would prove a hindrance to this mission.

5. Women and the State of the Counsels

Up to this point, we have deliberately spoken only of communities of men. The problem of the state of life takes a very different form for men and for women, first of all because, while there exist three possible states for men, women have two possibilities and also because the fact of natural virginity or non-virginity entails a differentiation for women that in turn is lacking for men. The fact that the priesthood is not a possibility makes the problem of the states of life easier for a woman, but the much more frequent occurrence of unwillingly remaining unmarried makes it more difficult. Especially in more recent times and as a result of the secularization of the supernatural idea of the states of life, the purely social state of being unmarried has drifted toward the supernatural state of consecrated virginity in a way that was previously unknown. On the one hand, this drift has led to a certain amount of unclarity, but, on the other hand, it has led to transitional stages from the secular state to the state of the counsels that are as yet unknown on the male side. The formulation of *Provida Mater* was surely prompted by female institutes, which are much more numerous than male institutes, and in the various associations of women a great deal of experience has been gathered that could point the way for male foundations. From ages past, Second Orders have stood alongside the First; but, next to the Orders of brothers devoted to schools and the service of the sick, there are far more numerous associations of sisters devoted to the same goals, indeed, for every form of charitable activity. The variety of constitutions and forms of life is as great as the variety of tasks. From solemn vows, to simple vows taken either for the whole of one's life or for a limited time, to an oath or a simple promise, once again for the whole of one's life or for a limited period, and from there to a simple association for some good purpose but without any further obligation—we seem to find an unbroken chain of possibilities. It is precisely this imperceptible transition that makes the distinction between natural and supernatural virginity or between the secular state and the state of the counsels so difficult: while for men, the only genuine possibility seems to be a clear synthesis of the lay state and the state of the counsels, with the one who remains a bachelor for religious reasons being a rare exception, there is a much greater danger for women of a blurred confusion. Here, too, we find a clarification in *Provida Mater*, which under the title of *Instituta sæcularia* includes all those who "follow the evangelical counsels with the aim of attaining Christian perfection and of fully exercising the Christian apostolate" in the form of vows, oaths, or a consecration binding on the conscience. These forms of life, in their stability, are taken to be part of the state of the counsels, and they are dependent on the Congregation for Religious, while all other associations that do not attain such a form of life are included within the worldly state. One would be glad to see this clarification help to bring about a similar clarification in the minds of Christians—not in the sense of a value judgment, but simply in the sense of a clean demarcation of the states of life and of the Christian laws of life that are valid in these states: the state of the counsels in the world is not the same thing as the secular state with inclinations to the spirituality of an Order (such as we find in the Third Orders) or with certain customs and pious practices borrowed from the Orders.

As has been said, where women have already lived the state of the counsels in the world in a clear manner, they can point the way for communities of men. Their best example would probably be less the form given in the way of life founded during the time of the French Revolution: a life with vows, but in the bosom of one's own family and bringing together therein worldly occupations and religious practices; and more the form shown by the community founded by the Dutch Father van Ginneken, S.J.: a motherhouse with novitiate and studies, with religious habit, office in choir, and a group of contemplatives, where the individual members are sent out, after completing their studies, without any religious habit, to the various professions (this at least was the original plan of the founder), with the possibility that these members might be called back and with the obligation to return at regular intervals to the motherhouse for a certain amount of time. This achieves a harmonious equilibrium between being in the world and standing outside of it, as well as between action and contemplation; the woman who belongs to this institute can work in the midst of the secularized world without being untrue to the spirit of the counsels and without being hindered by a veil, but she has the support, which is so necessary for a woman, of a visible house that is her home and guarantees her stillness, relaxation, and recollection. For a woman who works apostolically in the world is even less able than a man to be left in isolation, without any tangible, concrete community. *Provida Mater* exhibited a deep knowledge of the human soul when it required all "secular institutes" to follow this framework. But as far as women are concerned, the possibilities that have thus been opened up are only beginning to be developed. We do not yet see any religious women working in the wide arena of secular public life; the form of their work and their habit prevent a complete identification with this milieu. We see unmarried women in the world dedicating themselves to all the works of charity both inside and outside the Church, but these activities, however admirable and indeed heroic they may be, do not form an ultimate unity with the person's form of life; they can be given up at any time, for example when the woman marries or for the sake of another activity. They are certainly the expression of personal goodwill, but they are not what they would be in the state of the counsels: the expression of a mission accepted in obedience. Here, too, the intended synthesis is still missing: where the secular profession would be the expression of spiritual obedience, the total Christianization of the secular sphere with the total form of the state of perfection.

Conclusion

What is sketched here does not pretend to be a quick solution to the problems of today's Church. It wishes only to indicate *one* path that could be taken, a path that, precisely because it emerges from a reflection on the central structures of the Church, also touches on some central practical questions when it is followed. For we ought to seek to hear the Christian answer to contemporary problems, not from the secular sphere, but rather from the innermost essence of the Church herself—but this is the Church in her supratemporal youth, producing from the old tree trunk ever new embodiments of her divine-human life. Because her life is more than natural, it is not subject to the morphological laws of history. This is why we see in her the miracle that the earlier great foundations of Orders, all of which were necessary and modern in their own period and were given by the Holy Spirit then with the intention of being an answer to the pressing concerns of their own present day, nevertheless do not get old, are not superseded, and are not overtaken and left in the shade by those Orders that are modern today. The monasticism of the Benedictines, the Franciscans, and the Dominicans is completely alive today, for these great foundations are divine and therefore participate in some way in the mysterious eternal youth of the Church. They are ways of living out the gospel, the imitation of Christ; they are ultimately ecclesial forms of the continued Incarnation of the Word, and this is reason enough for them to retain their exemplary value for all subsequent generations. But this does not prevent new times from demanding new answers and new solutions, solutions that do not supplant earlier ones, but rather aid them, interpret them, and inspire them, as the last note of a melody to be played explains the previous notes and makes clear the unity of the whole melody. But it is only at the end of time that the entire melody, as it was composed by the Holy Spirit and unfolded through the centuries, will be complete and thus fully comprehensible. It is the task of the present day to grasp as purely as possible the note that must be played today, the divine word that must be spoken today, and to incarnate it as obediently as possible.

PART TWO

THE EVANGELICAL COUNSELS IN TODAY'S WORLD

I.

THE ESSENCE AND SIGNIFICANCE OF SECULAR INSTITUTES

The publication in 1947 of an "apostolic constitution on the canonical states of life and secular institutes for the attaining of Christian perfection" was an event in the Church whose significance can scarcely be overestimated. The number of secular institutes seeking approval in Rome in the years that followed rose like a mighty flood: the requests increased from fifty in 1949 to 210 already in 1953. In the appendix to his foundational book *Les Instituts Séculiers* (Paris, 1954), Jean Beyer, S.J., lists nearly ninety institutes, some already approved and some seeking approval, including twenty-nine in France, fourteen in Italy, thirteen in Holland, nine in Spain and in Germany, six in Austria, two in Switzerland, the rest in other countries.[1] A further forty-three names and addresses are found in the *Documentation Catholique* of August 21, 1955. As superabundant as these lists may seem, they give only a very imperfect picture of the impetus of the movement as a whole, which is perhaps even more fundamental and certainly more widespread than that of the mendicant

[1] An overview of the German-speaking countries is also given in *Herder-Korrespondenz*, December 1955.—Cf. A. Timmermann, *Die Weltgemeinschaften im deutschen Sprachraum*, Der neue Weg, 2, Schriftenreihe für Weltgemeinschaften (Einsiedeln: Johannes Verlag, 1963).

Orders in the Middle Ages. Despite tough resistance from the ranks of the older Orders, at a relatively early stage the Church granted a Magna Carta to this movement, a legitimate framework and a clearly defined theological and canonical space within the structure of the Church's states of life; and she has continued to show herself a truly provident and far-sighted mother, as the opening words of the fundamental constitution *Provida Mater* (PM)[2] rightly say. The theology in this document and in the accompanying ecclesiastical texts, which has been articulated with perfect clarity, and the praxis to which it gives rise are so bold that not even the best ecclesial theologians of our time have caught up with it, much less sounded out its depths. Even less could we say that the broader Church, the religious, priests, and laity, have realized the significance of this event. Focused on their goal, the institutes do their work in silence, often in a state of total hiddenness. It runs contrary to their nature to make any public advertisement; likewise, they are little interested, perhaps

[2] Text of *Provida Mater* (PM) (February 2, 1947), of the important motu proprio *Primo feliciter* (PF) (March 12, 1948), and of the instruction *Cum Sanctissimus* (CS) (March 19, 1948) in AAS 1947, 114–24; 1948, 283–86; 293–97. Also, with detailed commentaries, in: *De Institutis Sæcularibus documenta Pontificia, necnon studia dogmatica, iuridica, historica, practica* (1951), and in: *Enchiridion de Statibus perfectionis*, vol. 1 Collectanea S. Congregationis de Religiosis, 1, (Rome: Officium libri catholici, Piazza Ponte Sant' Angelo 28, 1949). Translations in Beyer (very accurate); Bonne Presse, in *Schweiz. Kirchenzeitung* (reliable); in the appendix to my book *Der Laie und der Ordensstand* (Herder, 1949) (some errors in translation).—Cf. also the revised translation in *Die kirchlichen Urkunden für die Weltgemeinschaften* (*Instituta Sæcularia*), collected by Jean Beyer, S.J., foreword by Hans Urs von Balthasar, Der neue Weg, vol. 1 (Einsiedeln: Johannes Verlag, 1963).

too little, in fashioning their own "theology"—which is no easy task, since it opens up the inner core of the entire structure of the states of life in the Church and requires that we reflect on it—but it is all the more necessary that such a task be undertaken. It is not possible to broach such a vast theme in this article; a few summary indications, which would need to be amplified at every turn, must suffice.

Let us recall once again at the outset:

1. Our starting point is not projects, hypotheses, or bold proposals that might be dangerous and must be accepted with caution, but a fact regarding the Church—a fact of such weight and momentum that every educated person must pay heed to it.

2. The ecclesial authority has not only already given this fact its approbation, but much more: it has provided a fundamental theological elaboration and evaluation of this fact and has determined its place in the framework of ecclesiology; it is sufficient here to reflect on the words of the Pope and of the competent Roman congregations, especially the Congregation for Religious (to which the institutes are assigned), and to let these words sink in.

1. The Fundamental Idea

The "counsels" Jesus gave to those who sought "perfection" beyond the keeping of the commandments: to "sell everything" (Lk 18:22), to "leave house, brothers, sisters, mother, father, children and lands" (Mk 10:29; Lk 18:29), to "remain unmarried for the sake of the kingdom of heaven: he who is able to receive this, let him receive it" (Mt 19:12), and thus be already now "equal to angels and sons of God, being sons of the resurrection" (Lk 20:34–36), ultimately to renounce the free disposal over one's own self in "following me", obeying (Mt 19:21, 27) and "giving an account of all that one has done" (Mk 6:30); these counsels or special callings, which are clearly marked off in the Gospels from Jesus' commandments—such as the command given "to all" to "take up his cross daily" and "lose his life" (Lk 9:23f.), or the command to love enemy and neighbor, which becomes quite simply the identifying mark of the Christian as such (Mt 5:43f.; Jn 13:34–35)—belong to the inviolable foundation of the historical religion of Jesus Christ. Despite all the variations that the following of Christ's counsels has taken in the course of history, the Church, who "from the beginning of Christianity has striven with all her power through her Magisterium to state clearly this teaching of Christ and of the apostles" (PM 2), has held fast to the counsels as a step and a decision that once and for all profoundly determines the entire form of life of the Christians who accept them, something that transposes these Christians "into a kind of order and public state of life [veluti ordinem classemque socialem], which, under the most diverse names, has been clearly recognized and repeatedly confirmed" (PM 2). The Church will never depart from this structure in which Christ's counsels establish a "state" of life, any more than she will ever depart from her hierarchical structure (with the duality of "clergy" and laity as something that establishes "states" of life); both of these distinguish her from the church of the Protestants, which in principle knows no states of life.

According to PM, the core life according to the counsels of Christ is the "total handing over and consecration of one's life to Christ [plena deditio et consecratio]" (2) in a "total dedication that is not hindered by any other ties [in plena nullisque aliis vinculis limitata deditione]" (8), pointing here above all to that voluntary virginity consecrated to God which first introduced the life of the counsels into the Church but which, as history has shown more and more clearly, fundamentally includes the other two counsels as well.

The question facing us today, which has become urgent because of the way culture has developed in the modern age and the way Christian life and its committed involvement in the culture has developed, is this: Can a life according to the counsels of Jesus Christ be brought into unity with "life in the world", in a secular profession with its rules and obligations, that is, the life of a normal lay Christian, or does the life of the counsels absolutely require one to leave the world, to surrender one's professional work to be free to dedicate oneself exclusively to the tasks of ecclesiastical life and service, as a "cleric" (in the usual sense)[3] or a member of a (contemplative or mixed) Order or of a religious congregation? By approving the secular institutes, the Church has answered this latter question in the negative. One can enter the "state of the counsels" by "*leaving the world* [relicto sæculo]"; until now, and "since the age of the Constantinian peace"

[3] The fact that the form of the secular institute is also open to the *diocesan clergy*, and has already been eagerly adopted by this clergy, interests us less here and will therefore be passed over.

(PM 3), this was the only form of the life of the counsels recognized by the Church as establishing an ecclesial state of life. "But in his great goodness, the Lord, who takes no heed of persons and summons all the faithful ever anew to lead the life of perfection and to follow perfection everywhere, has ordered things according to the wonderful counsel of his providence in such a way that *even in the world*, subject though it is to the plague of innumerable vices, a great number of groups of elect souls have come to blossom and are still coming to blossom, especially in our own days. Not only do they strive for personal perfection: they remain in the world, thanks to a special divine vocation, and have discovered excellent new forms of association that correspond best to modern demands, in which they can lead a life that is extremely well suited to the attaining of Christian perfection" (PM 7).

Primo feliciter (hereafter PF) also explicitly and repeatedly emphasizes the significant phrase "even in the world", warning against every tendency to assimilate the form of life of the new institutes, however slightly or however unconsciously, to that of the old Orders and congregations. The communities that lead "the life according to the evangelical counsels in the midst of the world" (PF 1) must "continuously see to it that the specific and distinguishing mark of the institutes, namely their *secular character*, which is the entire basis of their existence, necessarily be visible in all things [character sæcularis, in quo ipsorum existentiæ tota ratio consistit, in omnibus elucere debet]. *Nothing whatsoever is to be subtracted from the total profession of Christian perfection*, which is firmly established in the evangelical counsels and which constitutes the essential core of religious life. But *this perfection must* be lived and established in the confession of faith *in the midst of the world*" (PF 2). The Pope takes this even farther; indeed, he takes it to the farthest possible point, when he says, with full consistency, that the apostolic form of life is "to be lived out faithfully *not only in the world but, as it were, emerging from the world* [non tantum in sæculo, sed veluti ex sæculo]" (PF 2)—since being *in the world* "continually nourishes and renews" apostolic zeal and the desire for an ever more complete gift of self. And the apostolic form of life must insert itself into the world, adapting itself to the demands and conditions of the world, "in all that is permitted to a Christian". The institutes are to enter so definitively into the world that they are radically cut off from any dependence on existing forms of monastic and religious life: "The regulations of canon law for the state of religious are not applicable to the secular institutes", but this does not prevent the latter from "being reckoned among the states of perfection that are legitimately regulated and recognized by the Church" (PF 5).

2. *The Layman in Today's Church*

When the Church thus expanded the form of life in the counsels of Jesus, it is not that she was finally doing something she had failed to do earlier; rather, she was simply keeping pace with the development of the world and of its culture, which has entailed a number of shifts in life in the world and in its structures.[4] The culture, which

[4] On what follows, see *Schleifung der Bastionen*, 3d ed. (Einsiedeln:

in past ages had a deep effect only on the work and lifestyle of a very restricted group of people, has a hold on virtually everyone today. Since even the simplest man enjoys the "benefits" of scientific progress, he becomes indebted to it; he is taken up into broader sociological contexts, and his work becomes something performed in these intellectual, rationalized systems; he shares, whether he wishes to or not, in responsibility for the totality. This intellectualization of life goes hand in hand with specialization, and all coworkers are assigned a particular task, which they must take seriously and cannot approach as a dilettante. This may run the risk of curtailing their wide-ranging freedoms but compensates by raising the level of their personal responsibility. Specialization means competence, which is acquired through professional study and the experience of professional life; it is an intellectual treasure that cannot be replaced by anything else, not even genius. It is no longer possible today for anyone to have a proficient, comprehensive overview of all areas of specialization. Philosophy thus finds its role drastically re-

Johannes Verlag, 1989; Eng. trans. *Razing the Bastions* [San Francisco: Ignatius Press/Communio Books, 1993]); *Der Laie und der Ordensstand* (Einsiedeln: Johannes Verlag, 1948; 2d ed., 1949; Eng. trans. in first part of this book); "Der Laie und die Kirche", in: *Sponsa Verbi, Skizzen zur Theologie*, 2 (Einsiedeln: Johannes Verlag, 1960), 332–48 (Eng. trans.: "The Layman and the Church", *Explorations in Theology*, vol. 2: *Spouse of the Word* [San Francisco: Ignatius Press, 1991], 315–31). *Die Gottesfrage des heutigen Menschen* (Vienna: Herold, 1955; Eng. trans. *The God Question and Modern Man* [New York: Seabury, 1967]). An enormous bibliography is gathered and annotated in Yves Congar, *Jalons pour une Théologie du Laïcat* (Paris: Cerf, 1953).

duced; henceforward, it is limited to a relatively formal aprioristic knowledge of certain fundamental laws of the world and of existence, whereas the task increasingly falls to the individual sciences to fill out the substance of these laws through their investigations and results.

Considered from a purely secular and sociological viewpoint, however, this also affects theology in its position as the concluding and crowning science; it has become a "department", a "particular science" alongside many others, and there exist only two possibilities for the theologian, no matter how high he may stand in the Church's ministerial office, to speak meaningfully and successfully to the laymen who are involved and specialize in cultural work: either he must remain strictly within his own professional field (that is, that of understanding and interpreting the revelation of Jesus Christ in light of its sources) and attempt to present it to the general public (in the commission, and with the special assistance, of the Holy Spirit); or else he must lay down for the laymen the most general of guidelines, drawn from revelation, for the sphere of their own professional work and life. But as soon as further questions arise within the specialized situations of the laity, the laymen themselves must be summoned to answer them, and in such a way that they are always taken seriously as those who have the irreplaceable experiences that can come through the very exercise of the function that is inextricably bound up with the culture, or through an intimate connection with that function.

This makes it clear that it is not merely the "evil times" that prevent the clergy from penetrating as effectively into social structures as they did in earlier ages; and thus that, if the clergy, which is no longer able to accomplish its task, calls on the help of the laity (as happened in a big way for the first time in Pius XI's Catholic Action) so that they, too, can collaborate in the Church's apostolic tasks, it is not due merely to a state of emergency. One can indeed speak of a vicarious role to the extent that this lay help is determined by a negative state of social and religious affairs that prevents the clergy and the old Orders from reaching the milieux in question; but to the extent that this inaccessibility is caused by the normal development indicated above, the layman who lives and works in these social milieux is not compensating for the clergy and religious but is in fact carrying out his proper apostolic function. The fact of his baptism and his confirmation authorizes him to carry out this function, which is rightly his own, so that he does not need first to be charged with a special mission. While it was the first aspect of lay work that emerged more prominently in the period of the last pontificate (that of Pius XI), it is the second that is emerging more and more clearly in practical and theoretical terms in the present pontificate (that of Pius XII), without thereby abolishing the first and portraying it as invalid and superseded. It is clear that this autonomous apostolate[5] of the layman, too, must be carried out in the proper spirit under the regulatory supervision of the ecclesiastical hierarchy and its directives. But as a *lay* apostolate, it has its own special form. It is not primarily a dogmatic, theoretical proclamation, but rather the efficacy of one's whole existence, the example that

[5] This word is masculine (*apostolatus*), as is "primacy".

is lived out, as a pervasive yeast, a pervasive irrigation, a pervasive illumination both of the secular material sphere and of the secular social milieu—from one's own family, to one's friends and colleagues, and perhaps even to those who can have a decisive influence at some point on the milieu, the subject, and the area of knowledge and activity.

Thus it can be said that the apostolate of the laity is predominantly one of working inside the world and its structures and relationships, as opposed to the apostolate of the clergy and the old Orders, which is and remains an apostolate from above and from outside, bringing the Christian truth to the world and perhaps also living out Christian perfection for the world in an exemplary manner outside the world (*relicto sæculo*). Whereas the latter are prepared and sent out for their task through an emphatic *uprooting* from secular relationships and structures, a sociologically visible break from them, laymen are prepared and sent out precisely through their being *rooted* in these same secular relationships and structures. People speak, rightly, today of an apostolate through one's "presence" (par la présence) in one's own milieu and of an "intense Christian renewal of families, professional work, and civil society through intimate daily contact [impensam familiarum, professionum ac civilis societatis christianam renovationem *per contactum intrinsecum et quotidianum*]" (PM 10), which—as is now becoming ever more forcibly obvious—cannot be replaced by any other form of apostolate and is therefore *primary* and indispensable in its function.

This is why there has been an increasing and ever more

urgent demand for a "lay canon law", a formulation of the particular jurisdictions that would correspond to this autonomous lay function and protect it, one that goes beyond what is formulated in the present ecclesiastical code: only this would guarantee a wholly satisfactory collaboration between clergy and laity.[6]

3. *The Analogy of the State of the Counsels*

Unfortunately, the theme we have chosen does not allow us to examine in detail the question that arises from what we have been discussing, namely, the question of lay piety; we shall return to this briefly in the concluding section. The question we must address now is how the position of the Christian layman in the world, as defined here, can be brought into a unity with the evangelical counsels "fully lived out" (PM 12), "without any reduc-

[6] "I venture to take the view that as long as things remain like this (i.e., as long as the juridical question has not made any progress), we will never have the kind of Catholic Action of the laity that we desire. Genuine responsibility and obligation will be assumed and borne only where one has . . . in principle a certain area of freedom, *juridically* guaranteed, for the autonomous execution of these duties and tasks. As long as the layman in Catholic Action is only one who carries out the will of another—even if this is a priest or bishop—without any autonomy of his own, we will wait in vain for a Catholic Action that would include immediate collaboration with the clergy and the hierarchy, with the active involvement of more than just youthful idealists and pious old busybodies, or those in whose case the difficulty mentioned here is papered over by an accidental personal relationship of friendship and trust to the relevant ecclesiastical authorities": Karl Rahner, "Über das Laienapostolat", in *Schriften zur Theologie*, vol. 2 (Einsiedeln: Benziger, 1955), 350.

tion" (PF 2); we have seen in the first section *that* the two are compatible. It is in fact not easy for one who knows the history of the state of perfection and has grown up with a conventional view of the Church to see how it is possible, and it seems no easier for the clergy and the theologians of today.

The field of vision of the constitution *Provida Mater* is wide enough to include, in theme and explicitly in its title, the entire "state of perfection" and thus also lays out, both historically and systematically, the interrelation between its subdivisions: "De statibus canonicis institutisque sæcularibus christianæ perfectionis adquirendæ". The historical development, which is briefly sketched out, runs in two directions: first, there is the full development of the form of state of life that reached and maintained its culmination in the great Orders with the profession of solemn vows; then, in the modern period, there is the increasingly magnanimous adaptation and assimilation of other, less strict and less publicly visible forms to this paradigm. First, after sharp conflicts with the old Orders, came the recognition of simple public vows as an equally total form of self-gift, initially as a privilege for the coadjutors of the Jesuits and, finally, after even tougher resistance had been overcome, under Leo XIII (*Conditæ a Christo*, 1900) for all congregations with simple vows; then, recognition was further extended to societies without public vows that live according to the evangelical counsels, such as the Oratorians, Vincentians, and Sulpicians (1918, in the Code of Canon Law, bk. 1, pt. 2, tit. 17). Finally came the secular institutes in 1947.

In order to understand these two developments in their

simultaneity—the constant growth beyond the forms of the old Orders, and yet the constant reference of the new forms back to the old "paradigms" in which they "participate"—it is necessary to draw a clear distinction between the perspective of canon law and the theological (or essential) perspective. The former takes the fully realized form of the old Orders as a kind of measure and model to use in its juridical assessments of subsequent forms. And since this "*paradigm*" of religious life denotes de facto *also the richest and therefore the unsurpassable expression of the life of the counsels in the order of ecclesial representation*, that is, in its making sociologically visible an essentially supernatural and thus also eschatological ideal in the visible Church,[7] it is quite correct for all subsequent structures to order themselves (also in ways that go beyond the juridical) to this paradigm. Thus, newcomers will have to ask themselves: Do we possess the spirit of the praise of God as the Benedictines display it in their prayer in choir, the spirit of poverty as the Franciscans represent it, the spirit of obedience as the Jesuits practice it?, and so on. But alongside this indispensable reference backwards which is more than a polite bow before the past and before the presence of the old Orders in our own day, *Provida Mater* also displays a clear impetus forward, coupled with an equally strong impetus to look to *the origin of all the forms: the gospel.* It is the gospel, not the old Orders, that represents the absolute and unique standard for measuring

[7] And indeed the whole period of the Middle Ages in the broad sense (from Constantine to the baroque period) was predestined to this also from the sociological perspective.

the idea of the special Christian following of Christ—in all the variations of the one state of the counsels. Thus we come more and more to an *insight into the essence* of this life, which cannot consist in anything but the (ecclesiastically recognized) following of the three counsels of Jesus; it is less important whether this takes place in a contemplative or an active life, whether the gift of one's life is made through a solemn vow or only a public and simple vow or, indeed, merely through a private vow or, ultimately, without any vow at all, but only through an oath or a promise; whether this takes place in a monastic community that, because of its cloister, is clearly visible or in a looser community, one that may be somewhat visible or one that is virtually invisible, with members living singly in the world; or whether—the decisive point for us here—the vows are lived by means of a decisive, visible step out of the secular structures or by remaining within these structures.

But if these distinctions become secondary in relation to what constitutes the essence of this life, what then *is* this essence, which is common to all the forms and in which they encounter one another, not merely analogously, but univocally and *on equal terms*? According to *Provida Mater*, it is the total and unlimited consecration of the entire person and the whole of one's life to the Lord, as stated at the beginning of the text ("plena deditio illimitata"), in the same totality and immediacy with which the first disciples and women gave themselves to the Lord: according to the explicit teaching of Paul in 1 Corinthians 7, this remains the better form in relation to marriage and possession and autonomy. (This scale of values belongs to the defined faith of the Church: Council of Trent, session 25, canon 10.) This is the consecration that binds one to Christ as bride to the bridegroom, and this is why it excludes marriage, which is "*only*" a single sacrament, whereas consecration means the participation and immersion of one's whole existence in the total or primal sacrament of the mystery that relates the Church as Body and Bride to Christ the Head and Bridegroom, and in such a way as to form a free, personal act that therefore includes "poverty" and "obedience".

The important consequence of this is that the mode in which each "counsel" is lived out needs to be measured, not against the way it is lived out in the old Orders, but rather against the archetype of the following of Christ, as this following can and should be reflected in the concrete ecclesial situation. If we are talking about the situation of the layman in the world, the divergence of the ways it is lived out will be much greater than, for example, the differences between the old Orders taken individually. Just as it would be no recommendation of an institute to say that its aim was to imitate Carmelite contemplation as closely as possible, so it would be no recommendation to say that it strove to adopt and copy Franciscan poverty or Ignatian obedience in their material forms. To adapt does not mean to "compromise" here; such compromise was explicitly excluded by *Provida Mater*. Nor does it denote a kind of fluid "transition" from the spirituality of the Orders to that of the laity in the ecclesial "state of life in the world". Life in a secular institute is not "easier" than in Carmel or among the Trappists; it is not less radical, only radical in a different way. And yet this new state of life[8] forms a bridge between the two "halves" of the Church, which are so tangibly separated from each other by the "departure from the world" of the clergy and religious. It does not form a bridge by borrowing certain traits from either state in order to melt them together into a new, third state of life. Nothing is borrowed; it is a particular embodiment of the following of Christ—something that up to now has been the privilege of those who departed from the world—within the world, in the sphere of the "layman".

4. *Significance for a Theology of the Church*

This possibility—which has been a reality for a very long time—has profound implications for the theology of the Church's states of life and thereby for the structure of ecclesiology as a whole. To get a sense of how urgent the problems are in this area, one has only to compare what we have been saying here with the whole series of well-known and significant proposals that have emerged in our age, and one cannot fail to note the discrepancies.

Though these proposals may differ from each other, for the most part they share something in common: they

[8] The reality is not as new as we have laid it out here, for simplicity's sake. It is at the same time a new instantiation of the great medieval lay Orders: the Templars, the Teutonic Order, the Order of St. John, etc., and of many lay movements (e.g., the Devotio moderna) that strove to live the counsels of Jesus in spirit and often in reality, in more modest and freer forms, without a strict monastic rule. One should also note how often such freer inspirations stand at the origin of movements that subsequently led to the firmly established Orders.—Cf. the first part of the present book, above.

attempt to carve out a theological *locus* for the layman-in-the-world in a more conscious and determinate way than before and to unfold his essence. Typically, this occurs by setting the sphere that belongs to office and "structures" in a relative antithesis to the sphere that belongs to "life", the existential sphere. Yves Congar's well-known ecclesiology reduces the tension between clergy and layman to this simple polarity. Although this theological proposal is not to be rejected in every respect, its weakness is that it makes the antithesis between clergy and laity too central to its thinking and, consequently, does not leave any original place open for the state of the counsels. But the state of the counsels is clearly a "*structure*", since it is the state of life in which the following of Christ is lived out in a representative manner for the Church as a whole, and yet it is decidedly "life", since it embodies in a preeminent manner the subjective holiness of the Church —in antithesis to the objective holiness of Christ in the Church, which is administered by the clergy. This is why (in view of Congar's theology) I have sought to anchor both poles of the tension explicitly in an overarching common ecclesial basis (*Muttergrund*) (Mary as archetype of the whole Church and, therefore, also of Peter and his office, although Mary herself is not a priestess in the hierarchical sense). On this, see my essay "The Layman and the Church".[9]

We could raise a similar, though even stronger, objection to the proposal Karl Rahner sketched out in his essay "On the Lay apostolate" (*Schriften zur Theologie* 2:339–

[9] See note 4 above.

73). In his endeavor to help the layman attain the special character and autonomy that belong to him in the Church, he has developed a system that a priori refuses the layman-in-the-state-of-the-counsels any possibility of existence.

Rahner defines the concept of layman *negatively* in contrast to the nonlayman, which means:

1. In contrast to the "clergy", those who bear hierarchical authority through ordination (*potestas ordinis*, priests) or through being entrusted with a part of the *potestas jurisdictionis* as something the bearer possesses as a *habitus*, something that sets its seal on his existence. (In addition to the priest, "clergy", in this sense, would include the nonpriest who serves the Church, for example, one who earns his living as a catechist or a professor of theology or someone who helps in parish work—thus the concept certainly includes women, too. It also embraces the "laymen" employed to help the clergy in what is properly called "Catholic Action".)

2. "In contrast to the religious and members of the *Instituta sæcularia*, because these, too, vow to live the evangelical counsels". Only the subsequent *positive* definition of the layman makes it clear why these latter are not included among the laity: for whereas "clergy" and "religious" (both in the senses defined here) are of their very nature obliged to take *a step out of the world* in order to enter upon their office, their ecclesiastical professional work—the religious in such a way that they "are the expression, the visibility, the representation of a very specific essential characteristic of the Church, namely, the fact that she has both her origin and her end in something that transcends

the world: . . . the eschatological grace of Christ"—the layman, on the other hand, is characterized by the fact that he *remains in the world*, in the particular historical situation, rooted in the context of the secular structures that need to belong to the kingdom of God and be redeemed, with a "secular office" that only he can carry out. Considered ecclesiologically, he possesses this position (a) as a full member of the holy Church; (b) as one who is baptized and thus shares actively in the celebration of the eucharistic sacrifice, one who is given the sacramental commission for this office in confirmation; (c) as a potential and actual bearer of charisms that are assigned directly by the Lord of the Church and cannot be made subject to the ministerial office, but must be taken seriously by this office; (d) as one who is sent, one who bears responsibility, since both of these are included in Christian existence as such; and, finally, (e) also *jure humano*, since he is capable of taking on certain functions (such as godparent or administrator of the church building). The layman does not need to be given a special new mission from the clergy for any of this. The clergy has its own special ministerial apostolate *within the Church*, and it becomes capable of this apostolate first of all by its fundamental renunciation of any rootedness within the world: as the gospel shows, the office-bearer is stamped by his origin, his "whence": he is snatched out of his place in the world; he has abandoned his secular profession, his nets, his clan, his family; he lives from the altar; he is poor, unmarried, without a stable dwelling; he is freely available (as Paul's relationship to his young assistants shows), so that he can be put to work anywhere. His goal, his "whither", is to be sent, in his office, "throughout the world", before kings and foreign peoples. What he carries is not his own person but the gospel, cutting straight through all the structures of the world; he thus provokes discomfort; he becomes the object of suspicion and is persecuted. His apostolate is "aggressive", and it can be aggressive because it has its origin in a place that lies outside, indeed, above the world. The layman's apostolate is precisely the opposite. The Christian layman bears witness to Christ in the place in which he is rooted, not through the proclamation of doctrine, not through direct publicity, propaganda, addresses, and conversions, but primarily through the example of his life, the silent and consistent total Christianization of the *secular* task entrusted to him as father and mother of a family, citizen, scientist, artist, and so on. "Beyond this, he has no apostolic task." To prepare himself for his specific task, the layman must therefore primarily deepen his interior spirituality, not go into "training to become an intrusive soldier in the Salvation Army", for that would be "a symptom in the Church of a sickness born of the totalitarian spirit of the age". For subtler nuances and gradations, we would have to read Rahner himself.

We cannot avoid leveling the serious charge that this notion[10] with its purely eschatological grounding of the state of the counsels, removes any possibility a priori for bringing together the state of the counsels and the lay life. From this perspective, to follow the counsels of Jesus means to be uprooted from the world and to renounce

[10] This concept corresponds to the typical way of looking at things that we find today especially in Germany and in the sphere of influence of Ernst Michel's writings.

any work in the world. "Leaving everything" and following Christ entails the sacrifice and cross of renouncing the natural position that belongs to a person by inheritance, thus making him capable of the "sixtyfold and a hundredfold" fruitfulness over the whole world. In the grace of Christ who calls and sends out, giving up one's "unique situation" in the material context of the world results in the ecclesial universalization of the apostle. One may think here of Paul, of Francis Xavier. But there are several other things we would have to consider:

1. The narratives of those called in the Gospels appear to justify Rahner in the very close association he makes between the vocation to office (clergy, ordination, apostolate) and the vocation to a life according to the counsels; the apostles of the first period are in fact the representatives of both states of life. But, there are also women. There is also the rich young man, and the friends of Jesus; soon afterward, there are consecrated virgins, ascetics, and so forth. On the other hand, we have the married clergy. To make the clerical state (that is, the administration of the Church's objective means of salvation) and the state of the counsels (as living out the subjective basis of salvation) converge with one another accords somehow with an ideal view of the Church, but the real point of convergence does not lie at all *in* the ideal Church (which is feminine, without any office: Mary), but *above* her, in Christ. He alone is the objective, official high priest *through* his subjective personal sacrifice.

2. The guiding image of the apostle at work here is one-sidedly drawn from the Pauline-Ignatian perspective. The danger of absolutizing this image is that we would

identify the "hundredfold" fruitfulness of the apostolic work of the one "uprooted" with his freedom from the world, his distancing from matter, and the restrictions of concrete situations, so that his fruitfulness would be based on the Platonism that Rahner elsewhere so detests.[11] It is of course true that the old type of Order corresponds to this guiding image. It is only because the Jesuit is detached from the world that he can be totally available to the pope and to his religious superiors, who are in principle unrestricted in the use they may make of him. And, because this initial break from the world is never rescinded, it remains true that *this* universality can *never again* be reinserted back into the structures of the world. The most it can do is approach the world in an infinite asymptote, until it reaches the point of almost perfect imitation. Peter de Nobili takes on all the mannerisms of an Indian monk, Schall of a Chinese mandarin, but both remain ready at any moment to do and to be something completely different, at the slightest word of the General. In the same way, the Jesuit state in Paraguay was never a real state but only a deceptive imitation, and the heart-rending problems of obedience that led to its destruction clearly reveal its inner nature. A state that can be "revoked" by the Church on any given day is assuredly no state. The question is only whether this exhausts the idea of a *special* apostolate. Could one, for example, reduce John and

[11] Besides this, since the old Orders stand squarely within the line of representation and "making visible", the "hundredfold" would be seen from the viewpoint of apostolic "productivity". But the personal consecration of the one who vows obedience to God (in the Church) cannot be *instrumentalized* (objectified) in this way.

the Johannine apostle to this (Pauline) archetype? And what do we do with what Rahner calls charism, which he explicitly attributes to the layman? Does not the call to follow Christ in the form of one's life bear clear charismatic traits (1 Tim 4:14; 2 Tim 1:6)? Or, on the other hand, does not a powerful and demanding charism in the sense of a (lay) task in the kingdom of God lay claim to the *whole* of one's existence and thus require making one's life available in the counsels? And why should this charism, this *particular* task, deriving directly from God, not be a task that lies within the structures of the world, so much within these that it would be wholly impossible to carry it out by any "departing from the world" like the old Orders?—for example, the task of a Christian author, artist, journalist, editor, politician, doctor, or lawyer? Is it not simply false to suppose that a person has greater supernatural effectiveness in the kingdom of God the more he is removed from the unique historical (and this always means secular, world-historical) situation? Is Walter Dirks not much more correct (in his exceedingly rich book *Die Antwort der Mönche*), when he describes the great charisms, which were bestowed in the course of Church history on the founders of Orders and their work, as supernatural phenomena (and correspondingly "suprahistorical", lived out publicly in the "city on the hill") indeed, but as possessing an inner-worldly goal in *world* history, which the Holy Spirit himself intended? Is this not the only way to rid ourselves of the fatal risk of turning the Church into a *civitas perfecta* alongside the world, with her own functionaries and laws, a *civitas* that indeed (and unfortunately) comes into contact with the world, that other *civitas perfecta*, through its *members*, but that in itself leads its own life and lives its own history?

3. Should we not extend this line of reflection and say that it is perhaps the specific task of our generation, which is so strongly conscious of the positive significance of the historical situation, to realize that there does not exist, or need exist, any antithesis between apostolic universality and being rooted in history; and to realize also that God's kingdom, which (as Church) is coming, has nowhere else to come but *in the world*? It is certainly very beautiful when a Francis Xavier rushes swiftly through Asia and "lays claim to" peoples and lands for Christ. But a little flag planted on the summit of a hill is not yet the transformation of the wilderness into cultivated terrain. And yet who achieves this transformation? Must one not give very serous consideration here to the earthly *stabilitas loci* of the Benedictines: only presence in an earthly (and thereby historical) place can set a Christian mark on the terrain, the earth, the population. Do the parables of the Gospels not use very organic images to speak of the kingdom: growth from within, out of the earth, through the planting of the seed in the field, so that it is buried, puts down roots, and ripens patiently? And is not the hundredfold fruit the fruit of the *earthly field*, rather than the fruit of the sower, who has "left everything" in order to sow? It could therefore be important that *Provida Mater*, in addition to the common word "apostolate", uses other synonyms, such as "penetration" and "contact", and in addition to the aspect of renouncing the world speaks of "consecration" ("*consecratio* et instrumentum valde opportunum *penetrationis* et apostolatus . . . per contactum

intrinsecum et quotidianum", PM 9–10). Indeed, *Primo feliciter* refers explicitly to the evangelical gifts of grace to the apostles: they are to be

> *salt* for a spiritless world, enshrouded in darkness, a world in which they cannot participate but in which they nevertheless must *persevere* by God's design. They are to be *light* . . . and finally *yeast*, which, though invisible, is effective and which carries its effects everywhere, at all times, mixed into every strata of society, the lowest and the highest, striving to reach them all and to permeate [permeare] each and every one through word, through example, and in every other way, until it has so totally permeated the entire dough that it rises up in Christ as a whole. (PF, introduction)

One should not forget in this connection that, for contemporary man, the *stabilitas loci* has become very relative: places, firms, and branches are changed much more easily than in the earlier age of a culture of farmers and artisans. Thus establishing a layman in the state of the counsels in one particular secular post is no longer so "tragic", something that ties him down for the whole of his life: the secular situation itself is taking on some traits of "uprootedness", with the increasing intellectualization and universalization of culture and of its means of communication.

The points indicated here may perhaps not penetrate people's consciousness as long as ecclesiology is written predominantly by clerics and members of the old Orders, who not infrequently incline unconsciously to measure the ecclesial state of the counsels against their own image and likeness, as this has been preserved through the centuries. By the same token, the vital and existential experiences of the secular institutes are only just beginning; the shaping of the evangelical counsels for the situation of the laity in the world poses many questions that are (and must be) in principle soluble but that have not yet been tested sufficiently in detail; this is why they have not found their final formulation. Perhaps they admit a greater variety of responses than in previously existing Orders, especially with regard to the counsels of poverty and obedience.[12] But we must hold fast to one point: the members of the Institutes do not belong to the "clergy" in Rahner's sense—unless perhaps we think of them at the same time as standing in the situation of the layman, as Rahner describes it, which is impossible according to his conception.

5. The Layman in the State of the Counsels and the Layman in the Married State

We conclude with a brief indication of the significance of the "new" state of the counsels (1) for the situation of Christianity in our age, and (2) in particular for the situation of the married layman in the Church.

1. Bringing together the lay state and "evangelical perfection" sets up a bridge that, for the first time in the Church, allows those in the lay state (in this context abstracting from the lay brothers in monasteries or from religious

[12] We cannot discuss these difficult particular questions here. For the time being, cf. Jean Beyer, *Les Instituts séculiers*, p. 2: "La Théologie des instituts séculiers" (93–99). Cf. also my essay, "Das Ärgernis des Laienordens", in *Wort und Wahrheit* 4/7 (July 1951), 485–94.

congregations like the brothers who work in schools and hospitals) no longer to appear fundamentally as second-class citizens, belonging to a state that is ultimately not capable of full "perfection". And indeed, taken as a whole, the possibility that there be men wholly consecrated to God penetrating into all the Christian and unchristian states of life and living in them without separation and distinction, toiling, suffering, and bearing fruit in them, is a new possibility full of undreamed-of promises. The coincidence here of an eruption of charisms (one may think of the communities Father Voillaume founded and of many communities in Rome as well as in Italy and Spain more generally) with the promulgation of such a far-sighted Church law bespeaks an almost unprecedented *kairos* in the Church. The institutes can do things that neither the clergy nor the old Orders could or can do—not merely de facto, but also (as we have seen) de jure. The layman in the state of the counsels has the possibility of transforming the structures from within. Besides this, being unmarried gives him two potential advantages over the Christian and the non-Christian married man: more time and more means. He need not use his "leisure" for his family but can dedicate it to the Christian and universal concerns of his profession and his professional organization, for example, questions of professional ethics (in theory and praxis), which can increasingly be adequately formulated by those within, by the lay people trained in the profession. Nor need he devote his material earnings to those dependent on him but can use them—especially where larger communities and groups come together—to meet the needs and carry out the tasks of Christian culture and social work for which no one else has money today: neither the Church (as everyone knows) nor the secular authorities, who tend to support anything but projects with a "confessional" link. The number of the cultural obligations of Catholics that have been left undone in this way is legion. Everyone may imagine for himself what the presence and the influence of such men, who live exclusively for God, could mean in every aspect of all the professions and layers of society.[13]

2. The second question is more important in this context: what this new type of lay Christian implies for the state of life of the rest of the laity. This new type is significant first of all in overcoming the overemphasis on the bipolarity between clergy and laity in the Church. One could in principle also seek to overcome this in Rahner's way, by resolutely including among the clergy all the lay people (women as well as men) who are consecrated to God in a special and habitual manner and serve, while, on the other hand, compelling the formulation of a canon law specifically for the laity. But the way ecclesiology has developed seems to suggest another path. As we inquire more and more insistently into what the juridically distinct forms of the state of perfection have essentially in common and consider them from the perspective of this common element, the emphasis on the (external)

[13] If one scarcely ever encounters this effect as yet, this is in part because there are still hardly any significant institutes of men, and the female institutes are often only somewhat freer variations of previously existing congregations for education, the care of the sick, help in parish work, etc. Thus the statistics are deceptive.

"leaving all things" takes on less importance vis-à-vis the (internal) consecration of one's life, which of course *finds expression* in virginity, poverty, and availability (as Thomas Aquinas already knew: the vows as "perfectionis effectus et signa": *Contra Gentes* 3, 130) but is not simply identical with these forms. This was always clear and true, since according to the universal teaching of the Church (which only follows the gospel here), perfection consists in Christian *love*, which is not a *counsel* but rather a commandment that obligates everyone and is therefore capable of being fulfilled substantially by everyone; thus what the counsels require of one can only be an expression of love, a path to love, a more direct path, the radicalism of love's exclusiveness, something that appears as the normal and in fact the necessary expression precisely in the case of a *particular* vocation to particular love with a particular commission. Although this has always been certain, it has not always been evident to the same degree. If the perfect expression of perfect love is the following of the counsel, but this counsel consists in the *external* act of leaving all things, then it is difficult to see how the one who does not leave all things externally can truly attain perfect love. This picture changes as soon as the center of gravity *within the state of the counsels itself* shifts to the inner personal consecration. For now the married layman, too, receives a genuine, intrinsic connection to the meaning and substance of the counsels. It thus becomes clear what it means to tell him that the counsels are meant for everyone and that everyone must observe them, either literally or in spirit (1 Cor 7:29–31). We can also see why Ignatius in his Exercises leads all who strive for perfection to the point of *indifferentia*, which lies between the two ways of living out the counsels: "pobreza asi actual como spiritual" (no. 98); in this respect, perfection—to the extent that a man can strive for it and achieve it—lies, *not* in the material act of "leaving all things", but in the active readiness, the unconditional *fiat*, which is essentially the same as personal consecration. For from this perspective there is no reason why God's act of calling and sending out could not also place a man (once again) in a secular post, in such a way that, *out of* obedience, he now must take on the free responsibility of a layman for a portion of the world and, *out of* poverty, he must take on the administration of a portion of material or intellectual possessions and goods. If it is not possible, *out of* virginity (and while remaining in virginity), to enter into marriage, it is due to the limitations of the bodily-fleshly situation of our mode of existence, and perhaps it would not be entirely wrong to say that it is due to our postlapsarian relationship to the body, which is affected by original sin and no longer belongs to paradise.[14] For the relationship between Christ and the Church as Bridegroom and Bride is at one and the same time virginal and bodily, as we see in Mary, who is simultaneously Virgin and Mother.

As the representation of *this* mystery (and not merely the eschatological aspect of the Church), what unites the other states of life is the state of the counsels, particularly as they are lived out by the layman in the world.

[14] Cf. Michael Müller, "Die Lehre des hl. Augustinus von der Paradiesesehe und ihre Auswirkung in der Sexualethik des 12. und 13. Jhs. bis Thomas von Aquin", in *Studien zur Geschichte der katholischen Moraltheologie*, vol. 1 (Regensburg: Pustet, 1954).

According to the statements of *Provida Mater*, the consecrated lay state stands as a distinct state of life between the two others ("media inter clericos et laicos": PM 4), but its central position is of a peculiar sort, since, on the one hand, the distinction between clergy and laity proceeds from the essence of the Church, *insofar as* she is a *visible* "hierarchically ordered society", while, on the other hand, the "middle" state, to which both clergy and laity can belong, must be acquired on the basis of a close and particular relationship *to the fundamental meaning and goal* (*finis*) of the Church (PM, ibid.). And this particular relationship to the depth and totality of the Church—which, once it is definitively established, will eliminate the distinction between clergy and laity because it will render it superfluous—comes to light with special clarity in the life of the counsels as they are lived out in the lay state, because here the two converge into one: the world's movement toward God and God's incarnational movement into the heart of the world, and also because the existential mystery of the sacramental structure (the mysteries between Bride and Bridegroom) is seen in its unity with the representation of that mystery as it is lived out in the world that is to be won for God.

Thus the married layman has an immediate contact with the consecrated layman. What the latter lives is a whole and comprehensive lay piety. The consecration to God, which he lives out through his adherence to the counsels of Jesus, is something the married layman can understand from the inside, something he can carry out in his own way. In his attempts to share in the spirit of the old Orders, he could get no farther than an external antechamber (in the "Third Orders"); in this new form, by contrast, a reciprocal openness and interpenetration of both forms of the laity becomes immediately possible and has often enough already been actualized. It would be possible for an institute to consist of a first, inner circle of members who live according to the counsels and a second circle of members who lead a family life. The same interests, the same goals, and the same spirit would bind them together. The secular institutes are not only an instrument for the missionary penetration of the world but are also to a certain extent meant to have an effect on groups of laity within the Church, on their spirituality, their self-confidence, and self-reliance. Only when this possibility of ecclesial life has come to blossom will we recognize how significant its absence was in previous ages. Whether this idea finds wings in our own country depends on the readiness of young people for active religious involvement—certainly, young people from all walks of life, but surely above all those who one day will be able and willing to bear a greater responsibility for their people and culture, namely, students.

II.

ON THE THEOLOGY OF THE STATE OF THE COUNSELS

1. The Scope of Today's Theological Evaluation

What characterizes the spirit of the Catholic Church to a great extent at this moment in history is a desire to be radical, that is, concerned with roots, thinking back to the origins; this is why she inquires into and seeks to illuminate the original content and the evangelical genuineness of all those things that continue to live on in forms that are more or less taken for granted. The questions touch on all aspects: Can the form of existence into which the Church settled at the time of Constantine and which has been assumed as the given point of departure for all reflection through one and one-half millennia in fact be justified on the basis of the gospel, or should it not—amid the crumbling of all sociological human structures—be promptly revised from the ground up? Another aspect of the same confrontation between foundation and history is the tension found in all strata of religious thought—theology, ecclesiastical praxis, ecumenical dialogue—between dogmatics and exegesis, between the "original" sense of revealed texts, which exegesis seeks, and their definitive ecclesial understanding; this discussion will not come to a close in the foreseeable future, and indeed perhaps can never be truly finished, but it has never yet in all Church history been carried on with so much passion. Whether the origin is looked on as "established" (the authoritative word of Scripture) vis-à-vis the changing ways the Church has embodied it or is, on the contrary, experienced as something "open", something that cannot be permanently fixed, vis-à-vis the tendency in history to become hardened and narrow all too quickly, the tension exists and gives rise, not only to resolute vitality, but in many souls to unease, uncertainty, and fear. The consequences tend in two directions: Modern man has grown accustomed to being offered handy formulae that he can grasp immediately; but if the Church and her theologians show hesitation, and they themselves seem unclear where exactly they stand, is not this a sign that their old edifice is shaky and that we would be wise to get out before it collapses? But, by contrast, have not those who have always been suspicious of dogmatic, juridical, and disciplinary regulations been proven correct today? Is the Church not in the process of a complete reform, relativizing all the rigid forms that she has adopted through the course of history? Should we not therefore hang on in the modern Church, since she is finally undergoing the reforms and reformations that others underwent centuries ago—unfortunately, without being able to convince Catholics of their necessity?

The state of the counsels, too, like everything else, is being subjected to the same X-ray examination. It has been cultivated and expanded widely by the Church's tradition, thought through and cared for with the utmost concern, and it has spread out in the course of the centuries like a mighty tree with a network of roots and twigs stretching farther than the eye can follow. But if one looks at it from a distance, in its totality, does it really correspond to the founder's intentions? Or has it merely held fast to certain fragments of these intentions, partly or totally obscuring even these through its one-sidedness or adulterating them with non-Christian thought forms and sociological trends? Should it not make us suspicious that it grew up and was acknowledged by the Church precisely in the period during and after the "Constantinian turn"? There may indeed have been isolated phenomena in the second and third centuries that prepared the way for this development—the historian's eye will always discern some kind of preparatory stages after the fact—but what is nevertheless more decisively important is that there was no "flight from the world", no hermitage, before Anthony, and no cenobites (that is, monks living together under a strict rule) before Pachomius. Often enough, people have recourse to sociological causes to explain the sudden outbreak of the Orders: the Church, which had seized hold of the world under Constantine, entered into and became deeply, perhaps all too deeply, immersed in the structures of the world, and she thus had to give proof at the same time of her nonworldly reality, call, and mission, of which she had such a vivid awareness during the time of persecutions. This would make the organized religious state nothing other than an attempt to correct a faulty development; being only relatively justified, it would thus stand and—considered more resolutely—fall with this development: since the intermediary historical forms are being relativized today, in the desire for an unmediated vision, from the perspective of today's historical demands, of Jesus' demand. And, for once, both demands appear to agree, since both aim ultimately at the world that is to be redeemed: a turning to the world with uttermost decisiveness and depth, and not at all a flight from the world that appears to be the fundamental slogan and the point of departure of all religious life.

For in fact the entire state of the counsels does seem to be subject to this one law—from Anthony and Pachomius via Basil in the East, Benedict and Bernard in the West, via Francis and Dominic to Ignatius and the modern Orders and religious congregations—no matter how strong the differences between the spiritual families may be and no matter how visible the tendency may be to correct the original contemplative flight from the world gradually through a more intense participation in the Church's apostolic action directed to the world. Yet the tendencies to apply the brake are still to be found: alongside Ignatius stands a John of the Cross, later a de Rancé, and (as we shall shortly show) both of these figures are contemplated and imitated up to the present day. They show in a pure form what remains present in the others, even if it is mixed and concealed: the beginning of the life of the counsels, which determines everything else, is the Egyptian desert with its isolation and its hermitages in which those words and deeds of pneumatic wisdom were spoken and performed that Palladius and Cassian carefully gathered together and handed on to the West. Here, they found their place in the rules and experiences of the Benedictine Middle Ages and still form the Jesuit novice's first and perhaps most decisive nourishment in tried-and-true, indestructible "guides to perfection": a kind of filter through which the gospel is sifted and which perhaps (who knows?) possibly neutralizes the most important ingredients right at the outset.

If this suspicion has once been kindled—and the suspicious voices have increased in number from the 1930s onward—then something else will be observed: the spirit of "Constantinian" monasticism, which is intimately connected with the sociological system formed at that period and which wandered with it into the Middle Ages and then on toward the modern period, has been and has remained more or less the dominant spirituality in the Church until today: it is the intellectual and spiritual life of the elite who formed "the good conscience" of the Church that had "fallen" into the world under Constantine and who were a living reminder for the laity (who were chained to life in the world) of the kingdom of God, of the "way it is supposed to be". If the laity received salvation sacramentally from the hierarchical Church, they received it spiritually from the monasteries: a connection with the spirituality of the Orders becomes possible and tangible in institutions like the "Third Orders" and later in Marian congregations and similar structures. The critical eye of the present is able to discern the historical conditioning not only of religious life in general, but also of this secondary spirituality derived from it; and thus, taking up the corresponding Protestant demand made so long ago, it cries out for an independent, original interpretation of the Sermon on the Mount conditioned by the existential situation of the Christian in the structures of the world.

This presupposes a positive reevaluation of secular

structures by dogmatic and spiritual theology (something yet to be achieved), irrespective of whether a life according to the evangelical counsels is compatible with a daily lived contact with these structures. Many well-known contemporary theologians are endeavoring to reflect anew on all the aspects of the very same "world" that many a celebrated early Christian and medieval tractate said one should flee from and despise (*despicere*, *contemnere*). These theologians view the "world" in a light unknown until now, namely, as the summation of the reality Christ redeemed and the object of the Church's co-redemptive and missionary activity. Whereas a religiosity of late antiquity could dovetail smoothly with the newly emerging Judaeo-Christian religiosity during the time of Constantine, it is only the post-Christian present day that offers an image of a wholly secularized world (J. B. Metz), of a universe that is visibly evolving into its own self and curving reflexively back upon itself (Teilhard de Chardin) with an array of autonomous problems, methodologies, intellectual concerns, and risks and rejecting any patronizing treatment on the part of a Church, a theology, or even merely a philosophy with theological coloring. The Christian can be the yeast he is meant to be in such a world only if he has matured along with the mature world and attempts to share in finding a solution to the questions of his professional work (which are known to him only, not to the clerical Church) on the basis of the bold responsibility of his own Christian conscience (cf. G. Thils, *Theologie der irdischen Wirklichkeit*, 1955). It is precisely in this real share in action that the true center of gravity lies, the genuine midpoint of the Church, where the yeast of the gospel comes into direct contact with the real world: in the mature layman, whose responsible, free, active involvement cannot be taken over from him by any ecclesiastical office, institution, or organization, no matter how spiritual it may be (Ernst Michel). Thus everything else in the Church must take its place as periphery around this center, as the means to this end: the proclamation of the Word, the administration of the sacraments, the organization of parishes and dioceses, the whole of the clergy that exercises these functions, but likewise, too, existence in the evangelical counsels, which possesses merely an "instrumental" significance: as an existential sign of the provisional character of temporal life, as a reminder of eschatology, of death, judgment, and the life to come (K. Rahner, and many others with him). This is the goal toward which the Church of the laity is striving in tandem with the evolution of the whole world—to be sure, the world takes a longer and more toilsome path, but it is just as noble and indispensable; indeed, we should probably say that it is in the long run much more important: for here the world sets itself in motion, whereas on the other path it receives nothing but gestured greetings from those who have abandoned it in all its distress and birth pangs.

Thus, what the monk lives out in obedience to an "abba" or superior as an "exemplary sign" has its real counterpart in the situational obedience of the mature layman who listens to his Christian conscience, to the summons of Christ that comes from within the secular moment: but in such a way that sign and reality in practice exclude one another. It is indeed very impressive when one man obeys another for the sake of the gospel; it is an ascetic practice that continuously reminds the Christian in the world how demanding it can be to choose the path indicated by conscience in the "situation". Yet the one who obeys another man cannot at the same time obey the secular situation in a fundamental and complete way. The mature layman in the world is in principle the man who experiences marriage: in the union of man and woman in the flesh, he has entered a spiritual bond that is so close and so demanding, though at the same time promising such a blessing—in an inseparably worldly and Christian sense—that life in marriage, understood and lived in Christian terms, appears as the fulfillment of what the evangelical counsels represent as a sign, in the same way, we could almost say, that the sacrament of the New Covenant of God's full Incarnation fulfills the prophecies of the Old Covenant, which were but words and signs.

The last decades in theology have brought a tremendously positive reevaluation of marriage; it almost looks as if it has been reserved to our age and the near future to explore the depths of this mystery, something we have only just begun to do. The investigation has, at this point, remained at the more psychological surface, while the ontological depths are still to be opened up. The mysteries of the generation of life, of fatherhood, of conception, of pregnancy, of birth, of childhood, of family, and of death in relation to these mysteries—what is surely the most important sphere of human existence has hitherto remained outside professional theology, possibly because the theologians, by virtue of their state of life, have no experience with it (and also forget that they themselves were once children). Does this not show once again that the real understanding of a reality depends on really having experienced it and that experience alone makes one competent to make compelling statements?

This seems to be what the hour calls for: genuine solidarity on the part of Christians with the world that curves back onto itself, that takes itself into its own hands, that molds itself. And the asceticism demanded of the Christian is not renunciation, but rather the appropriate, reasonable use of these goods and instruments, something that in some cases is a harsher demand than pure renunciation. It is more difficult to smoke less than not to smoke at all. And this example remains in the sphere of psychology, for smoking is not a necessity, whereas entering the married state, the use of temporal goods, collaboration in society, culture, and progress are things that nature commands and that God in turn insists on from the first page of the Bible: the increase of the race and kingly dominion over nature are an original obligation that will never fall away. Alfons Auer has shed impressive light on these matters (*Weltoffener Christ*, 1960).

Thus a spirituality that turns to the world is in keeping with the times; it is urgently demanded because it has been for the most part lacking up to now; it possesses the momentum one would expect, not least because it is a reaction against the thousand-year-long evaluation of monasticism as supreme. As a reaction, it will no doubt leap over its boundaries here and there; it will not be free of resentment against the old values and, therefore, will automatically call for the necessary counterweights. But the first thing it will do is relentlessly create space: space for the "normal layman" in the Church's life, space for his positive and indeed central position in the Church as a whole (since it is for his sake that clergy, preaching, and sacraments exist), space for his right to make his voice heard actively in ecclesiastical matters and for his participation in the total apostolate and priesthood of the Church (lay apostolate, universal priesthood). This movement is being promoted vigorously not only by secular priests (J. Cardijn, G. Philips, Thils, R. Guardini, X. Arnold, A. Chavasse, and so on) but with equal energy by religious priests (J. M. Perrin, Congar's book about the laity, K. Rahner, B. Häring, and so on). But it will also create even more space, in life in the world, where this shift in values will take place more easily and as a matter of course.

But this is to sketch only one-half of the present day. In a strangely harsh and extreme antithesis to this whole movement that we have sketched stands another movement, which amounts to a rediscovery of the most consistent forms of the state of the counsels. These forms were left in the shadows by the nineteenth century. The period between the Wars in the twentieth century began by bringing an enthusiasm for Carmel that reached wide circles. Thérèse of Lisieux was and still is a world event: her simple sentences about love for God and one's neighbor, her "little way" showing how this love could be realized, were a sudden revelation of the one thing necessary for a Catholicism that had grown gray and tired thanks to the culture wars, the syllabus, modernism, and neo-Thomism.

Thérèse's life was the breakthrough from a kitschy

Christianity to one that was radiantly pure, and her modest book was the document of this breakthrough; so, too, the effect she had was an unheard-of liberation for everyone—priest and layman and religious, adults and children, educated and uneducated alike. This unhoped-for light radiated out from the strictest Order of the Church, and if the Little Thérèse sometimes found her great founders, Teresa of Avila and John of the Cross, too "lofty" and, with a slightly malicious smile, set her child's path next to their eagles' flight, her smile had nothing ironical or distant about it. She had a profound veneration for her parents in the Order; she sought to interpret the meaning of Carmel in their spirit, outlining its essence in a couple of masterly brush strokes, simply and with greater clarity than even Teresa and John themselves could have expressed it. Alongside her, and almost contemporaneously, two other breakthroughs occurred, with rich consequences: Maurice Blondel with his spiritual diary and Charles Péguy with his rediscovery of the spirit of hope and of childhood. But it was Thérèse who led, seconded by a spiritual sister: Elizabeth from the Carmel in Dijon. At this point, the great works about John of the Cross (Baruzi, Father Bruno de Ste. Marie) and about Teresa (Oechslin, Waach, Auclair, and so forth) appeared, and Erich Przywara pointed with all his might to the spirituality of Carmel; inspired by him, Gertrud von Le Fort wrote her famous short novel about Carmel, *Die Letzte am Schafott* (*The Song at the Scaffold*), which Bernanos transformed, in an equally original experience, into the play *Dialogues des carmélites*. Claudel, too, counted his wonderful poem on the Great Teresa among his most important works, those in which he best expressed himself. In Germany, Edith Stein not only lived in an exemplary way the path from philosophy to Carmel and to martyrdom, but she illuminated this path and made it transparent in her writings.

But another light shone even more brightly in the period after the Second World War: the name of Charles de Foucauld became a central point around which many things, communities of all sorts, began to turn. This light, too, radiated out of an incomprehensible, apparently totally obsolete and irrelevant solitude. Foucauld began in monasteries, then was only a hermit in the Sahara, taking the path of the forms of religious life with ever greater radicality back to the origins, to Anthony the Great and, behind him, to the gospel. He, too, like Thérèse, was a completely simple and childlike soul who plunged back, from the banks of the "institution", into the living, life-giving, and fecund spring. But this is the same spring that Thérèse discovered: the pure *caritas* of the Gospel, as yet undifferentiated into pure love of God and pure love of neighbor; Foucauld was the man of perpetual eucharistic adoration and biblical meditation and, at the same time, the one who naturally took care of the poorest of the poor who besieged his hut in the wilderness. He drew up from the well of his contemplation pure *caritas*, as yet untouched by any cultural garnishings: the immediate response in gratuitous love of the whole man to Christ, whether he is encountered in the sacrament or the Word or in his neighbor abandoned in destitution. In his "Little Brothers and Sisters", what Foucauld brought to the poor was the poor, naked life of pure love, which bore witness only to itself: deprived with those who were deprived, captive with the captives, helpless with the helpless. Foucauld chose the material desert as the sign of this poverty, and his followers began by establishing their novitiate in the same Sahara, but the sign played only a modest role in face of the reality: the wilderness is everywhere, and those who have come afterward find it just as genuinely, though more brutally, in the factories, in the black kraals, in the slums of the great cities. This relativization already allows us to look ahead to the meaning of the evangelical counsels in our time. Foucauld drew up a sketch, in which he attempted to root the multiplicity of the ecclesial forms of life in the life of Jesus himself, who lived the first thirty years of his life as a normal worker in his family and his secular profession, then spent forty days in the desert as the one who vicariously adored God and was vicariously tempted, and finally worked for three years (or even less) as the active apostolic proclaimer of the kingdom of God—it is not possible to extend this reflection and understand the Passion as a "form of life" that can be imitated, for it is something that is bestowed, something that radiates from above into all three conditions and permeates them with its form: life in the world, pure contemplation, and ecclesial apostolate. Seen in this way, none of the three forms would have any advantage over the others, but it would be demonstrated that all three are genuinely founded in the gospel and compenetrate one another in the unity of Jesus' existence. What this immediately implies is that each one, taken individually, can be interpreted only on the basis of its interweaving in the unity, so that the eremitical life and pure contemplation (for example) can be understood only as integrated into the total organism of Jesus' existence and, hence, of existence in the world. Here Foucauld meets up with a fundamental idea of the Little Thérèse, who had understood Carmelite existence totally as vicarious representation for the Church and for the entire world. But this is to anticipate the expositions that will be given later.

Besides Thérèse and Foucauld, we should mention a third person who is little known outside France, one who faced constant opposition and solitude and followed untrekked paths. Abbé Monchanin tried to construct a bridge between Europe (with its Christianity) and Asia by entering into the conditions of an Indian contemplative and building for himself there a mysterious interior path to the hearts of his brothers, while the paths and methods of external missionary work largely failed. Why can Asiatic contemplation not be a pathway to the absolute and, thus, to the true God? For there cannot exist two absolutes. Why not accompany these brothers on their path, as they grope toward God with so many sacrifices, praying with them instead of speaking to them, living—existentially and not merely strategically—in the same poverty and renunciation that they take upon themselves, in order to find the one pearl of great price? This is a path on which the courageous man could be followed only by a few (Raymondo Panikkar, Matthias Vereno, and J. A. Cuttat have tried to make this path more comprehensible to us), but here Monchanin's steps are not far from those of Thérèse and Foucauld, who were just as unequivocally concerned with "God alone" and the "souls of their brothers" in God. The dilettante's talk and practice of yoga, which have become fashionable in Europe, are in general far removed from Monchanin's path, for they consist for the most part in forms of self-seeking (spiritual or psychological hygiene): yoga remains a means to an end, not a form of total Christian commitment. But it is such a commitment that is needed if there is to be a genuine encounter with what Asia has held onto in its depth and can still offer to Europe in its confusion. And here (as J. A. Cuttat rightly emphasizes) we cannot help but turn our gaze to the connecting link between the continents: to the Christian East, to Byzantium, Syria, Armenia, Kiev, and Moscow, to the holy starets on Mount Athos, and to the origins of monasticism, which are indissolubly interwoven with the theology of the Greek, Latin, and oriental Church Fathers. And is it not the case that the Church Fathers remain for *all* time Fathers of the Church, who can never be repudiated? Their theology after Constantine is not essentially different from what it was before. Almost all of them led the life of the evangelical counsels; many were monks before becoming bishops or teaching theologians.

Europe, Russia, and America can use their machinery externally to trample down Asiatic contemplation and perhaps destroy it, leaving only scattered remnants; but this does not in the least mean that it is spiritually overcome, still less assimilated. And spiritual values cannot be killed. They rise again, strengthened by persecution and resistance, and issue the challenge to a just and honorable duel. It would be short-sighted and dangerous to dismiss Asiatic contemplation as something undeveloped that had not even risen to the level of Greek thinking (a common charge in Europe, for example, from Hegel onward), or as a form of thought that (as Teilhard de Chardin held) will be automatically superseded by the triumphal march of evolution. If this is not the case, if Schopenhauer at least in a formal sense raises a genuine objection to Hegel, then Asia, too—quite apart from the gospel—remains a constant exhortation to Christendom to pay heed to what represents at least *one* aspect of the one thing necessary.

2. *The Gospel and the Counsels*

a. *Theology of the states of life*

In the midst of the stream of our age, surrounded by various forms that presume to be taken for granted, let us, too, attempt to find our way back to the origins out of which they have grown and which alone allow us to understand them.

If it is true that God himself has turned to humanity in the biblical event of salvation of the Old and the New Covenants, most supremely in Jesus Christ, speaking to humanity and dealing with it, finally becoming incarnate and entering into humanity, then we have an initial consequence that precedes all else: it is impossible that God, who is essentially infinite, wholly other, and incomprehensible, should enter into the web of human concepts of order through his speaking, dealing, and becoming incarnate in such a way that he can be grasped and comprehended. Rather, in this event, all inner-worldly univocities will break open in order to offer as far as possible a space and a vessel for the freedom of the Almighty.

Neither the Word of God nor Jesus nor the Church nor Christian existence can be reduced to an all-embracing and comprehensive definition: *Si comprehendis, non est Deus*. Herein lies an infinite wealth of meaning, which takes the breath away from the one who contemplates it: endless vistas, all of them accessible, lead toward a glowing, unapproachable center. Who can say definitively *how* the divine and the human are related to one another in the word of the Bible (no matter how precisely we know and how often we indeed see *that* they are distinct from one another)? It is at any rate not the case that the one begins where the other stops. Who can say definitively where the divine and the human natures meet each other in Jesus, how they collaborate, what is to be attributed to the one nature and what to the other? The mystery laughs at every attempt to master it. Who dares to define in concrete terms what in the empirical Church has a divine origin and what a human origin? For example, what in the Church is the mystery of human rebellion against Christ's commandments, and what is the mystery of a profoundly hidden share in Christ's suffering through and under human weakness? What is the penance she does for her own guilt, what for the guilt of humanity outside her? The same question can be asked in regard to each individual Christian life.

Man can never reduce God and world, grace (supernature) and nature to a relationship that he can survey from above, for otherwise he would be a third, synthesizing entity above God and the world. If this is so, then the Christian cannot even cobble together what he calls the natural law with the immediate summons that comes to him from Scripture and from Christ into a system that he can master: he may indeed possess the first law to some extent "in himself", but he will always stand "under" the second law. The same can be said of the Church: it is totally and a priori and forever impossible for her to reduce her own relationship to the "world" to a system that she herself understands completely and therefore can utilize to regulate, order, and select the steps she takes vis-à-vis the "world". Indeed—since she herself is a part of the world!—even in relation to herself, she cannot come clean, in the sense of being able to look at herself in a kind of architectonic blueprint and then begin to build herself up, giving preference now to one wing of the building, now to another, all in accordance with the comprehensive plan. She is God's handmaid, whose royal essence remains hidden and withdrawn from the Church herself for the duration of the world. She must continually listen to the Word of God in order to be able to communicate it further, and the more humbly she listens, the better will her proclamation be. All the more clearly will the "Lord, who is the Spirit", teach the "service of the Spirit" in this hour of history, too (2 Cor 3:17, 8). She does not have definitive recipes for every period of history, even if she has been entrusted with the total legacy of the Lord, which is valid for all time.

Nor may she let herself be deceived by formulae and slogans that at most show the general direction, without giving a clear definition of the position that must be taken. ("The Lord to whom the Delphic oracle belongs neither discloses nor conceals: he gestures", says Heraclitus.) What, for example, does "eschatological" mean?

Of course, it means "related to the end time". But is the end time in the future, or has this future already begun? Is the end time the present day? And in this case does not the one who leads an eschatological existence live in a manner absolutely corresponding to the law of his own age? According to Jesus, the kingdom is neither something that is to come only in the future nor something that has already come, but rather something "in the process of coming", and this includes and brings together both aspects in a mysterious way. Since the kingdom "is among us" as something existing now [*Da-sein*], the present aspect is at any rate very real, so real that it takes on a (third) aspect of the past, since it has existed—but this aspect is continually taken up into the aspects of the future and the present through the Parousia that Jesus promised, as well as through his Eucharist and his living word. The Bible calls this mysterious web of temporality, centered entirely on Christ, the "fullness of time".

The Lord calls men into this fullness, and he calls in two different ways, even if he calls both groups into the same fullness. He calls the small group of apostles in such a way that they are to "leave everything and follow him" in a radicality that forbids one to bid goodbye to those at home, to bury one's father, to look back once one has put one's hand to the plow: those called in this way stand beside him, removed from the family and possessions they once had, so that they can carry out their service together with him, as men commissioned by him, endowed with authority and power by him, and sent out by him; and, in the evening, after carrying out their apostolic daily work, they are to return to him to receive his judgment on what they have done (Mk 6:30) and to wait for new instructions. But only a small company is called in this way; the great majority are addressed in Jesus' preaching or encountered individually: sinners come; sick people come; they are absolved, cleansed, then sent away with a "Go . . .", back to their village, their family; sometimes even the wish of the one on whom grace has been bestowed "to be allowed to remain with him" (Mk 5:18f.; Lk 8:38f.) is categorically refused. Thus two movements of "eschatological" life come into being, from two antithetical positions, "states of life": some are called out, stand beside the Lord, and walk with him, following the movement of his Incarnation from the Father to the world, to men, in a Christian mission, in order then to return to him and find the pole of their rest in him. The others stand "in the world", but with the inner unrest that continually urges them beyond: looking to see where he might be, following him into the wilderness "like sheep without a shepherd", persevering, hoping, and giving thanks and praise when they have received something. Two circling movements: from God to the world to God, and from the world to God to the world; they go in opposite directions and intersect each other twice in the course of each orbit. Both movements are expressions of the same love, in which the one, unique perfection consists: the first is, as it were, at rest in itself, because the step toward God has been taken *formally* once and for all and must prove itself and demonstrate its substantial truth in each fresh departure and return; the second is more yearningly open, because everything on earth remains unsatisfying, since "the heart remains restless until it rests in you"—but when does it rest, other than in the brief moments of encounter that slake its thirst but end at once, when the Lord sends one away from him again? Both movements are unrest, and both are brought to rest: the apostle's unrest consists in the fact that the Lord sends him away (*apo-stellein*) into a world in which he is not and is not yet, and yet this unrest, too, is brought to rest, because the Lord himself is the one sent away from the Father to the world, and the apostle can only reach the people by travelling Christ's path to the world, by travelling Christ himself, who, as "the way", accompanies him precisely in his being sent. The Christian in the world, on the other hand, is restless because he wishes to find God in all things, which as such are not God: and precisely in this yearning search, he is made to hear, and also to feel, the blessing of those who hunger and thirst for justice. Thus things are in fact the opposite of what is usually supposed. Those "turned to the world" have taken their place once and for all beside Christ, to receive from him and together with him their mission to the world; those "turned away from the world" stand in the world and are made to feel its provisional character, its transience, its alienness, and are compelled to lift their eyes to God. On an initial level, the two movements are antithetical, and, viewed from the perspective of the gospel, nothing can change the fact that there are two "states of life" in the Church—if one understands this word, not in the medieval sociological sense, but wholly in its original biblical sense. The word itself is not important; it can be dropped if it is too heavily "burdened" by its medieval associations, and we are left with two "forms of life" (called *duæ vitæ* in the early medieval and patristic periods), which mean the same thing theologically, whatever name one chooses to give them. On a second level, the two movements touch one another in a most profound and multifaceted way, insofar as both allow a man—indeed, compel him—to exist in the above-mentioned oscillation between God and the world, the world and God, since both movements are circles that necessarily pass continually from one pole to the other, attracted and enriched by each but then led by each to the other, just as if God could not be found by himself, but only among men, and man could not be found among men, but only with God.

In Christian terms, however, this is not an empty dialectic, but the entirely concrete fulfillment of Christ's one, all-embracing commandment of love. In the New Testament, this is no longer put together out of two separate parts (to love God above all things and to love one's neighbor as oneself are the two Old Testament formulae [Deut 6:5, Lev 19:18] that Jesus is the first to join into one [Mt 22:37f.]), but these are integrated into one another (1 Cor 13:1; Jn 3, and so forth) insofar as God has become man. Because Jesus has atoned for the least of sinners, this man's sin is essentially present in the Crucified, and this is why the Crucified is in him and stands behind him. Thus whoever, as a Christian, approaches the least of his brothers walks toward the loving God. He sees precisely in the "least one" the veiled face full of blood and wounds—nowhere more intimately, more directly than here. The one closest to me is also the one closest to God. The sinner (you and I) is the one for whom God "died at the right time", namely, at the time when this sinner "was still his enemy" (Rom 5:6, 10), and this means that the state of being an enemy is, as it were, the sacrament of redemption, for here is the sign—the decisive, eminent, and effective sign—of redemption. The pagans love their friends; Christians love (also) their enemies. If there is a universal human "finding God in all things", insofar as all things speak of their Creator and—as Greek philosophy and the Bible unanimously declare—the heavens praise the glory of God, there exists also on a wholly new, infinitely more intense level a Christian encounter with God, founded on the hypostatic union and on the Cross, an encounter that finds the glory of God's suffering and dying love everywhere and, preferentially, in that which is far from God and opposed to God. But insofar as the Christian regards and addresses his neighbor in view of Christ, he already carries him in a creative way with him on his path back to God. The way forward and the way back are absolutely one and the same. This however presupposes the Christian love that "does not seek its own", the agape of renunciation and loving readiness. This love alone is perfection; this love alone, as we have shown above, gives the two formal, structured movements their meaning by filling them with content. Through love, the Christian "in the world" is summoned to selflessness and trained in it just as much as the Christian who answers the call to follow Jesus in an immediate way. If they are understood in Christian terms, the family and a secular profession are a hard school of selflessness. Parents serve their children, who finally leave them in order to marry, a law that is already proclaimed in the midst of paradise (Gen 2:24); the husband serves his craft or profession; the wife serves her household tasks; the child must go to school, in order later to serve as husband or wife. And the end of all this is always foreseeable, always threatening: precisely when the harvest is to be brought in, one must abandon it: "and the things you have prepared, whose will they be?" (Lk 12:20). At the very latest, death brings each man into the situation that the one called by the Lord enters in advance: total poverty, total chastity, total obedience. But we must also hope that the one in the state of the counsels has learned and carried out the movement to his neighbor until the time of his death in such a way that he has attained in total Christian selflessness the love that is (or at least can and should be) the hidden and often enough buried core of the secular state: as the spouses' total gift of self to one another, as the transparent love between mother and child, as the love of God that through Christ is hidden within all genuine human love, if it is willing to go to the end of love.

In the state of life of those called, it is customary to distinguish three counsels given by the Lord that place the man who follows them into the "state of perfection" (to whose definitive character the Church then gives her official recognition). Three additional explanatory sections are necessary here: (1) on the concept of "counsel", (2) on the differentiation into three counsels, and (3) on the content of each counsel.

b. On the concept of "counsel"

The explicit distinction between "counsel" and commandment is Pauline (1 Cor 7:25, and before that, in verses 6–12), but the notion itself is already synoptic (Mt 19:10–30 and parallels). Nevertheless, one must not overlook the fact that, in the real situation of the counsel, which is that of the rich young man, we cannot say for certain whether he is really "called" or only "permitted" to follow the Lord. It would scarcely be proper to apply the term "counsel" to the initial group of those called, since the words "Follow me!" addressed to the first disciples lay claim to them in such a sovereign way that they are left no time for deliberation and for collecting "merits" of their own; we see this even more clearly in the case of Paul, who *is* chosen and whose assent is already claimed in the act itself. This is why Paul cannot boast of his apostolate: "For if I preach the gospel, that gives me no ground for boasting. For necessity is laid upon me. Woe to me if I do not preach the gospel! For if I do this of my own will, I have a reward; but if not of my own will, I am entrusted with a commission. What then is my reward?" Paul gives the answer at once: "That in my preaching I may make the gospel free of charge" (1 Cor 9:16–18), that is, in a voluntary, gratuitous poverty that is not already contained in the poverty imposed on him by the Lord. "Counsel" is a relative concept, if we keep in mind both the voluntary character and also the constraint entailed in the Christian existence of every Christian. The sinner is not asked whether he wants to be redeemed: redemption takes place "at the right time, when we [all] were still sinners". Thus the sinner is confronted with a fait accompli, and if he recognizes this fact, then it is an "obligation" of free gratitude that he respond by making himself available to the Lord in his embrace of faith and baptism. But baptism, like the original act of redemption on the Cross, posits a "fait accompli" in him that goes far beyond anything he himself can experience and conceive: he is baptized into the death and burial of Jesus; he dies to the sinful world and rises again to the eternal heavenly world, and all that he can do, psychologically and existentially, is to limp forever behind this fait accompli without ever catching up with it. The only way to catch up with it would be to attain to perfect and definitively self-renouncing love: and yet, the attainment of this is, not a counsel, but the commandment that bears and includes all the others.

Thus, if one speaks seriously, the Christian has no choice about whether he will order everything—truly everything—to perfect Christian love. He must do so in a genuine decision, which can be made once for the whole of life, but must yet be repeated afresh, exercised, and given new life every day. (This is the fundamental meaning of the Ignatian Exercises.) In relation to this will for Christian totality, the question of one's state of life is utterly secondary; the decision to embrace the evangelical "counsels" depends then on the experience of being personally called (if this is lacking, it would be imperfect, indeed impious, to force one's way into the counsels and would be decidedly more perfect to choose the "secular state"); but in God's eyes, the readiness a man has attained to take this step (*if* God should wish it) is of equal value to the actual taking of this path in obedience. For the one who manifests such a readiness has placed his whole existence in God's hands so that he may dispose over it; he has renounced any autonomous shaping of his own life. He has given the preference to God, and thus he possesses love.

c. The multiplicity of the counsels

Are there many counsels? Perhaps; but there is nevertheless only one total gift of self, for the Lord makes the total demand of a life and receives this gift for his service, to be used as he wishes. The response of the one called, the one on whom a claim is laid, must possess the same total openness in the gift of self. What counts is the open *fiat* to the entire will of the Lord: unconditional, unlimited, not anticipated by human plans. No "Up to this point, and no further!", but: "Behold the handmaid of the Lord, let your word alone be done unto me. I am the matter, you are the form." This attitude has only one analogy: the indivisibility and indissolubility of the Yes given in marriage. Indeed, the gift of self to the Lord ought to be even more indissoluble, since it meets no boundary in death. If the Church does not count this total consecration of life (*consecratio vitæ*) among the seven sacraments, this is surely because what we have here is not, as in marriage, a symbol (efficaciously containing grace) of the archetypal union in love between Christ and the Church—as it were, a calling down of the primal marriage upon this particular marital union. Rather, here a man is drawn up into the unique primal sacrament itself; he chooses this archetypal sacrament (the union between Christ and the Church) as the immediate form of his life, and he receives it as his gift. He lives in the graced matrix of life that is the common ground on which all the individual sacraments stand. The consecration of his life makes him a *sacrum*, that is, something handed over to God and reserved for God's use alone, standing vicariously (with Christ) for humanity, something to be consumed for their sake and for their reconciliation, a burnt offering. This act of handing oneself over and being received is just as indivisible as Christ's sacrificial act for men vis-à-vis the Father. If one calls this consecration a "vow", the bridal character emerges even more clearly into view, and we can see that the one consecrated wins his privileged place in the heart of the Church, where she, as the Marian Bride, is "entrusted" for all her children "as a pure virgin to her one husband, Christ" (2 Cor 11:2). It is in this spirit that the nun receives the "veil" and the monk his habit, which hides him from the world.

Much more than in the marriage of the flesh, the entire fecundity of the bridal relationship to Christ depends on the indivisible *fiat*. In the marriage that images this bridal relationship, it is possible to separate the fleshly functions from the spiritual, but, in the archetype itself, never, since the entire fecundity of the sacrifice of the Cross for humanity depends exclusively on the indivisibility of the love of the Son of God. The sins were not the whole man, for they could be taken away from him and did not reach into the very end of human nature: this meant that they could not follow after the love of the Son, which accompanied him inseparably "to the end" (Jn 13:1). The womb for the grace-bringing divine Word is Mary's indivisible *fiat*, her total faith. Where we find "little faith", a faith that anxiously puts up barriers and makes arrangements in case it should turn out not to be true, or in case too much would be demanded, Jesus cannot perform any miracles (Mk 6:5). Above all, vicarious representation is not possible here, for everything that is restricted to itself remains private. The great harvest, which ought to be gathered in from the whole of humanity, does not reach a full ripeness. It was in this sense that Thérèse of Lisieux declared that the bridal gift of self that she made to the will and the love of the Lord as a Carmelite nun made her a "mother of souls" and set in motion the innermost engine of the Church, through which alone all the other actions of the Church's apostolate ad extra can become fruitful. Thus, Thérèse became patroness of the missions. This is of course a mystery that cannot be calculated by any statistics; this is why any way of thinking (outside or inside the Church) that judges by numbers and measures external success will evaluate the entire religious state as a luxury life of leisure without any sufficient purpose and will demand its abolition: in a violent sense, like the suppression of monasteries or through a milder ideological attack that portrays them as relics of an out-dated human culture, in which contemplation was thought to be higher than action. The fact that the one who lives according to the counsels of Jesus is no more able to demonstrate his successes than Jesus the Crucified himself could do belongs to the essence of the Cross, to its humiliation and shame, and thereby once again to the hidden fruitfulness of love's self-gift. No reality is more veiled than the love between Christ and the Church, and so the fruit of this love, too, which constitutes in God's eyes all the eternal value of creation, is hidden from the eyes of the world. Only indirectly and sporadically does something of this emerge into the daylight of general awareness: an exemplary holy figure who shines into the distance; a gesture of the Church that amazes the world and commands its attention, a gleam of holiness that wafts around the Church and that one would like to make one of her hallmarks (*nota ecclesiæ*)—though how much opposition and resistance this sign meets! But who can say whence these rays ultimately come? Which prayer, which act of self-giving was it that pushed its way, through trackless paths, into the outer sphere?

All this is to indicate the form and meaning of the consecration and vowing of one's life. Jesus points to this hidden dimension in the Gospels, when he imparts a counsel or gives a promise for "those who can hear". We can speak of a multiplicity of counsels in view of the objects of self-gift, since these are spread out into a multiplicity according to the essence and existence of the human being. There are the goods among which one lives—an external circle; secondly, there is one's own body and its highest, noblest function, that of the transmission of life—which is already a part of man himself; thirdly, there is his innermost sphere: self-consciousness, personal thinking, and creative freedom, that which is most inalienably one's own. It would be easy for the Stoic to give up the external zone, at most the second, too—but never the third. The same is true of Kant, for reason is autonomy. But the philosophers do not know the mystery of love, how it takes possession of the innermost realm of man and claims it for itself. It is already true in marriage that one partner has the right to dispose not only over the body of the other (1 Cor 7:3–4) but also over the whole person (since man is inseparably body and soul, and love has its seat in the soul), to the extent that this right is exercised according to the mind and the Spirit of God; but where someone chooses as the form of his life the mystery of the primal marriage between God and man, between the God-Man and the Church, he is opened up in all three areas of his life and "expropriated for the common good" ("exproprié pour cause d'utilité publique": M. A. de Geuser). Thus one must agree with Thomas Aquinas when he says that obedience is the most essential and most decisive act of the total gift of self (2a 2ae 186, 8). When one looks at objects that can be distinguished from one another and selects one limited area to make it the explicit object of the gift of self, this act must—at least implicitly—extend to the other objects, too. In the period before Anthony and Pachomius, there existed in the Church virgins consecrated to God, who lived in their families or in groups (somewhat like the Beguines today): they gave prominence to virginity as the special object of their consecration, but this included quite as a matter of course an attitude of poverty and the will to adapt themselves and make themselves available to the spirit, the directives, and the needs of the community as a whole. A total claim takes effect through all objects, thanks to the meaning of the consecration of one's life. This also allows us to understand why the two forms of life of the married state and the state of the counsels stand over against each other in a certain exclusiveness. For it would not make sense, nor would it likely be beneficial, for a married woman to make a private vow to her confessor concerning one of the three areas of life, since the power over these spheres belongs in principle to the common spirit of marriage and family that holds sway between the marriage partners. If this spirit is understood and lived aright, it already expropriates the individuals sufficiently and trains them in the gift of self. Thus one can say that the states of life ought not to be mixed, precisely because they are already adequately united in that which distinguishes them, namely, in selfless Christian love.

d. The individual counsels

If we consider the normal case, then, a person can vow his life to Christ in only one way, a way that embraces, offers, and consecrates the person's total existence. In this respect, it is better to avoid speaking of "three vows", since this obscures the existential substance of the indivisible act of the gift of self. Nevertheless, it is possible to look individually at the three areas mentioned, with the structures proper to each. This ought to make it clearer in what respect the two "states of life" or "forms of life" are bound together by the common Spirit of the Church and also in what respect they are set over against one another. The antithesis is immediately evident in the second, middle area: marriage and virginity. Here we have an either/or. Here—and perhaps only here. For who would prevent me from making my possessions available to all as something belonging to all, if not the law of family life? And who would prevent me from submitting my freedom and my decisions to a representative of the Church for the sake of Christ, if not once more the law of the gift of self in marriage, which lays claim to the innermost realm of the heart? Marriage and virginity are thus the "diacritical point". But here we find something quite remarkable: precisely what is incompatible for the ordinary man was held together only one superabundant time, at the very origin of the entire order of the Christian states of life: Mary is Virgin and Mother. As both, she is the fulfillment of Eve, who was a virgin in paradise and a mother after the fall, and who might—as many Church Fathers had profound reasons to suggest—have been both at the same time in paradise. Thus, looking ahead, Mary is the origin and foundation of both Christian states of life: quite explicitly of virginity (Lk 1:35), but also of marriage, since we cannot overlook her presence at Cana and under the Cross. She is Virgin and Mother; but considered more precisely, she is Mother because she is Virgin. Her virginity reverses the Old Testament ordering, in which marriage was seen as the fulfillment, and childlessness as shame,[1] but at the same time it fulfills the Old Testament ordering, because the act of faith demanded of Israel now demands her whole person, body and soul: virginity is the incarnation of absolute, unlimited faith, through the

[1] W. Hillmann, "Perfectio evangelica: Neutestamentlich-theologische Grundlagen des Ordenslebens", *Wissenschaft und Weisheit* 19 (1956): 162f., reprinted in *Das Wort, die Kirche und der Mensch, vier Kapitel zur urkirchlichen Verkündigung* (Einsiedeln: Johannes Verlag, 1964), 81–102 (now out of print).

act of the Spirit, in the flesh of Mary. *This* faith is the presupposition for the Incarnation of the Word of God, and, as presupposition, it is the response that is always already given to this Incarnation (since Mary is "proleptically redeemed" by the Cross). It is obvious here that one cannot understand the state of the counsels without Mariology, which is the core mystery of ecclesiology. Thus Mary is Mother because she is Virgin; the total gift of her person is the material out of which the Holy Spirit creates the new man who is the Son of God and who will redeem mankind vicariously through his total divine-human gift of self. Here we find an unexpected answer to many of the objections to the life of the counsels that we sketched at the beginning of this essay. Mary receives the experience of being a mother out of her total gift of self to God. The ultimate foundation for this experience is her virginity. And if Mary's virginal experience is the existential matrix in which all virginal life in the New Testament after her will have its roots, then this means at the same time that, when those who have vowed themselves to virginity receive the Marian grace, they also receive the gift of her experience of motherhood. For their gift of self to the Holy Spirit is not in the least something negative and private, as virginity always must be outside Christianity, where it is recommended for reasons of asceticism or hostility toward the body, or even given a sacral sanction (as in the case of the Vestal virgins). Rather, it consists in the limitlessness of love's gift of self, which exceeds even the natural limitations of human marriage and thus is the most positive and fulfilled thing that can be imagined on earth, in response to God's infinite revealed love. If this is the case, and Mary's limitless gift of self (or her total faith) is the presupposition for God's Incarnation and her experience of motherhood, then Christian married people will turn their eyes to the Virgin Mother in order to broaden their love from a limited human gift of self to the totality of Christian love, attempting to model their mutual gift of self after the archetype of her love, which is at the same time the core of the Church's love as Bride for her Bridegroom. In this way they will follow the apostle, who prescribes that they are to take as their model in marriage the mutual gift of self between Christ and the Church (Eph 5:21–33). But these same married people ought also to know that those in the religious orders are rooted in this same mystery, this same guiding star toward which they bend their necks; and that there can be no Christian Church without them, just as there can be no Christ without Mary. Everything in the Catholic Church's dogma is much more closely, deeply, and marvelously interconnected than many of the faithful realize and understand—to say nothing of outsiders. This is why little or no help is to be found from mere psychological reflections (about the spiritual effects of the life of the vows) or mere political or strategic considerations (about which form of life in the Church ought to be given predominance today).

If one looks from Mary to Jesus, a similar but perhaps even more hidden mystery comes into view. He, too, is unmarried; he, too, lives exclusively for his mission in obedience to the Father's will. But this exclusiveness includes everything: the whole of humanity is to be redeemed; the whole of humanity is ultimately to enter into the bridal relationship to him—through the mediation of the Church that he founds. For the sake of this mission, he leads a life of poverty and obedience. But since he is the incarnate Son of God, his relationship to humanity does not remain something purely spiritual: his surrendered, sacrificed body is drawn in the Eucharist *into* the eternal covenant. One cannot avoid saying that here, between the Lord and the Church, occurs the paradigmatic marriage event: here occurs the unimaginably intimate mystery of "uniting oneself to the Lord" (1 Cor 6:17) that makes "one spirit" of the two in the mystery of the eucharistic flesh. The Lord's surrendered flesh and blood is the origin of all Christian fruitfulness through the ages; it is the archetype and source of the consecration of life in the "vowed state". This bodily midpoint (where the spirit takes on bodily form and where external goods become a man's very essence) makes it possible to understand the form that structures the life of those who follow the Lord.

At first, the Lord takes his disciples just as Israel offers them: most of them are certainly married. It is only with Paul and John, with their example and their theology, that we first see the notion that one can follow the Lord also, and precisely, in virginity, in the context of the Lord's demand to leave everything, even wife and children (Mt 19:29). The Gospels do not show any conflict arising for the disciples here; nor do they show Christ breaking the bonds of existing families. Attention is drawn to the literalness of leaving everything, which refers initially to external goods (the fishers' nets, the tax collector's job) and includes leaving one's parental home. One cannot speak here of a mere symbolism or a purely "spiritual" understanding; if a "spirit of poverty" (and of virginity and of obedience) exists for all Christians afterward, it is because poverty has already been lived out in a real, material way: this is something that must be maintained against Luther and Protestantism. The Lord solemnly prepares for literal poverty as a possible form of life in those great promises that are like a foundational charter for both the poor, defenseless Church and for the life of the counsels within her: "Every one who has left houses or brothers or sisters or father or mother or children or lands, for my name's sake, will receive a hundredfold, and inherit eternal life" (Mt 19:29; Mark adds, "a hundredfold now in this time, although with persecutions, and in the age to come eternal life", 10:30; cf. Lk 18:29–30).

Virginity appears predominantly under the aspect of "counsel" because it cannot be demanded of everyone (although Paul would gladly do so: "I wish that all were as I myself am. But each has his own special gift from God. . . . To the unmarried and the widows I say that it is well for them to remain single as I do", 1 Cor 7:7–8; cf. Mt 19:12), while poverty appears partly under the aspect of a commandment, partly that of a counsel and recommendation (Mt 19:21). But obedience appears in the Gospels as the natural consequence of having left everything, for the one who has been thus summoned is now quite simply available (Mt 20:1–16; it is not for nothing that the parable of the workers in the vineyard follows immediately after the chapter about the counsels). The disciple's obedience to the Master is in the first place unambiguously obedience to a human being (who is recognized as the God-Man only in the course of time, later on; this does not abolish the bond of obedience between human beings, but only intensifies it). It is an obedience based on an acknowledgment of the spiritual superiority of the Master and his prestige but, at the same time, also his selflessness and humility vis-à-vis God. Accordingly, this obedience is understood implicitly from the beginning as obedience to God—more precisely, as training in obedience to God. Not only does the Master introduce the disciples into the kingdom of God and the disposition appropriate for it, as well as its laws and its prayer; he also praises and rebukes them, the latter often in harsh and unsparing tones; he gives them tasks, not asking but commanding them; he fills their daily program; he treats them like his subjects, like the instruments of his ideas and his commission. And since he does not do this arrogantly, but in humility, it becomes ever clearer to them how much he himself is one who obeys and how much their obedience as such is therefore the following of the Lord. But this is a following "after" him, not simply an accompanying of him, as if they, too, after being trained in a makeshift course of instruction, could gradually do without human obedience and "obey God immediately" as he does, rising, as it were, from an immature, mediated obedience to a mature, liberated obedience, be it an obedience to God or to one's own educated conscience or to one's total life circumstances in a "situational obedience". The disciples' paradigmatic, archetypal obedience to the Lord is and remains obedience from man to man in the clearest possible way; it remains a genuinely dialogical and genuinely incarnate obedience, which through the juxtaposition of two wills and two freedoms always keeps the person from believing he is obeying God when in fact he is ultimately obeying only his own self. The dialogical element of this situation cannot be eliminated, because the primal sacrament, which forms the ground of everything else, namely, the relationship between the Lord and the Church as Bridegroom and Bride, likewise always remains dialogical. Since this relationship has a clearly delineated structure in the life of the counsels, it makes sense to establish it as one specific "counsel" alongside poverty and virginity. But it is more their natural consequence, their radicality and consistency: whatever in the first two counsels is preparatory or negative here acquires definitiveness and a positive fulfillment: the one who has been made ready receives his directive from God; the vessel is filled with God's Logos, which is at the same time meaning-content and verbal command.

These observations, too, have absolute priority over any psychological consideration about what sort of healing or problematic effects such an interpersonal obedience might have and how it is to be understood and practiced in detail. Such concerns come later. But first, what we saw in relation to virginity must now be said about poverty and obedience: Just as Mary's (and the Church's) absolute virginal love and self-gift shines out from the foundations of the married love between spouses as an unattainable archetype and model, so the evangelical poverty of Christ and his disciples becomes visible at the foundations of every Christian relationship to worldly possessions, and the evangelical obedience of Christ and his disciples becomes visible at the foundations of every free Christian decision and fashioning of the world. This is what Paul means in his well-known directives: "From now on, let those who have wives live as though they had none . . . and those who buy as though they had no goods, and those who deal with the world as though they had no dealings with it" (1 Cor 7:29–31). Absolutely no Christian possession of the world or Christian fashioning of the world exists that does not also bear in its depths the stamp of the reality of the Christian life of the counsels, that is, of the disposition of Jesus Christ himself, which found expression in the Cross, and of the Yes that Mary said to the Cross. The "spirit" of the evangelical counsels is quite simply the spirit of the Church; the one who lives with the mind of the Church lives with the mind of agape, that is, of the selfless love that "does not seek that which is its own, . . . bears all things, believes all things, hopes all things, endures all things" (1 Cor 13:5, 7). There is no secular marriage, no secular professional work, that stands outside of the necessity of being borne in its most intimate depths by the greatness of this love that is in accord with God. The laity in the world often think little, or not at all, of the depth and comprehensiveness of this ecclesial love, which automatically differentiates itself into poverty and obedience: poverty, because avarice is counted by Paul among the gravest transgressions, and obedience, because every Christian ought to let himself be wholly formed inwardly in all his thinking, his aspirations, and his planning by the mind of his holy Mother the Church, the holy Bride of Christ, and ought therefore to listen constantly to her voice.

There is no other way to keep this disposition, which belongs to the whole Church, awake in the communities and in the hearts of individuals except by its being lived out in an exemplary way in the literal life of the counsels. The self-deceptions even for Christians are otherwise all too numerous, and the enticements too strong, in all three areas—worldly goods, eros, intellectual power, and freedom—with the result that many would succumb to them under the appearance of something good and useful: What could one not do for the kingdom of God on earth if one only made use of the means the world provides! The example of those who have made the renunciation in the vows keeps the salt from becoming stale in the Church as a whole; it does not constitute an authoritative precedent in a legal sense, but it is meant to keep alive the recollection of the Son of God's archetypal obedience. For the kingdom of God is not to be built through the instruments of worldly power, which are rejected in the temptation in the desert; only through the Servant's obedience unto death, even death on a Cross, is the world redeemed (Phil 2:8). This was assuredly an obedience to the Father who had sent him, but it also inseparably included an obedience to the authorities that God had instituted on earth: to the family in which he was "subject" for thirty years (Lk 2:51), even more to the "law of the Lord", which is identical to the "law of Moses" (Lk 2:22–24, 39), the last iota and dot of which had to be fulfilled, not only by the others, but by Jesus himself (Mt 5:18), in such a precise and total way that only the Servant of Yahweh was able to take on the full burden that, as Peter says, "neither our fathers nor we have been able to bear" (Acts 15:10). And how strict was Jesus' human obedience to the prophecies that outlined his earthly path in advance, although it is also perfectly true to say that these were made in view of him and determined by his sovereign mission: within time, they existed before him; he found them already in existence and oriented his activity and his being to them. All these human bonds were held within the comprehensive bond of the Father's will, which the man Jesus certainly experienced and felt to be "another" will: carrying out this will required him to renounce his own, "for I have come down from heaven, not to do my own will, but the will of him who sent me" (Jn 6:38), and therefore: "Not what I will, but what you will" (Mk 14:36), and: "Thy will be done, on earth as it is in heaven" (Mt 6:10), and: "I always do what is pleasing to him" (Jn 8:29), and: "My food is to do the will of him who sent me, and to accomplish his work" (Jn 4:34). In this obedience, he possessed his security, his dignity and inimitable sovereignty, and his exalted freedom, and he shone out as the only Son of God: here he was certain that he did "not seek his own glory" but solely "the glory that comes from the only God" (Jn 5:44). Such central statements allow us to sense how much Christ's obedience was a human obedience of renunciation, deprivation, and self-sacrifice, far from a "mastering of the situation" on his own by virtue of his own power and resourcefulness, and how much he listened in every choice to the wish and the will of the Father, who was "greater than he": "Truly, truly, I say to you, the Son can do nothing of his own accord, but only what he sees the Father doing" (Jn 5:19).

The Church would not be the Bride of Christ if she did not attempt to realize in her own life, through all her structures, something of this fruitful, salvific obedience. Every Christian is called to a visible and tangible obedience to an ecclesial superior, who has received something of the unconditional heavenly authority to issue commands. The laity tend to interpret this obedience in a minimalist sense—after all, there are very few declarations *ex cathedra*, nor are there many dogmas defined *de fide*. And yet this obedience, when interpreted in the correct manner, ought to be understood broadly: not as if every ecclesiastical declaration should be understood as a total or partial proposition of the faith—since that leads only to an externalization and falsification, which transforms genuine obedience into a literalism, and "the letter kills"—but in such a way that the believer, in all that he is and does, opens himself and listens to the innermost spirit of Mother Church and holds up this spirit (not some time-bound ideology, but the pure Marian disposition) as the rule of his existence and activity.

e. *Vows and office: The immeasurable mystery of the Church*

In obedience to the Church, the difference and the unity of the two ecclesial forms of life possess a peculiar mediation in a third form, the priesthood, which is initially neutral vis-à-vis the distinction between the only two forms we have considered up to this point, since it is possible in principle to have married priests in the Catholic Church, and such priests did in fact regularly exist in the first centuries. The priesthood is not primarily a form of life but an office that, as such, can be carried out in both forms of life but that the Church senses as having an affinity to the life of the counsels. This is not the place to set out and justify this affinity in detail; but it is not difficult to grasp it, if one reflects on the great proximity this office has to the office of Christ himself and also considers the practical advantages of the priest's being completely free for the community. Thus the form of life that the office-bearer usually possesses today is quite similar to the life of the counsels: celibacy is materially the same as vowed virginity, even if it is for the most part presented to the clergy in a somewhat muted way and recommended to them as something fitting: the priest's renunciation of marriage is also ultimately rooted in the one central mystery of love between Christ and the Church, and it also finds its support and sustenance in this mystery. Considered in principle, clerical obedience to the bishop is likewise not substantially different from obedience in the life of the counsels, although the one is ratified by an oath and the other by a vow. On both sides we find the same renunciation of self-determination, the same commissioning for the kingdom of God, although the work involved may take place in different fields. The secular clergy make no specific promise of poverty, but this is increasingly seen today as necessary, if pastoral work is to be fruitful and preaching credible and compelling. Without wishing to anticipate ecclesial developments, one could speculate that, if the future gives us married deacons and perhaps even (in emergency situations) married priests, too, the simple dyad of forms of life could be established in the ranks of the clergy, too: clergy in the secular state, on the one hand, with marriage and thus also with possessions and the right to dispose freely over them, and, on the other hand, clergy in the undivided state of the counsels, where explicit poverty (which is in fact often lived today already in the priesthood, in practice or in spirit) would then join celibacy and obedience.

It is clear from the original situation of the Church, from Jesus' association with his disciples, that the apostles had to embody the state of the counsels and the priestly office in the unity of their person. This means that not all those who follow them in the counsels must also exercise a hierarchical office, and the married state was seen very early on (in the Pastoral Letters) as compatible with the episcopal office. The later theologians of the religious orders liked to point out that the primitive Church in Jerusalem had a charismatic fellowship of goods (Acts 4:32–37), and thus here, in the unity of the person, we find the archetype of the ecclesial states of life that were subsequently to become distinct from each other. For Basil and many other Fathers, the state of the counsels was merely the attempt to relive, in a manner that would provide an example to all, what had once been the form of life of Christians in general. The observer will not find these manifold overlappings of the states of life an alienating confusion if he keeps in mind what we said at the outset: the Church as a whole can never get a comprehensive view of herself from the outside and can therefore never reduce herself to an ordering that strikes the natural eye as harmonious. The Holy Spirit of God is her innermost ordering principle, and this Spirit blows where he wills; his mysterious ordering often enough appears impenetrable to man. Thus, clear structures do emerge in the Church, as we have seen above, and certain centers exist around which logical forms crystallize; but all of a sudden we see that these centers, which are distinct from one another and cannot be gathered into a unity, are nonetheless rooted in turn in a single, common center, which gives each of them its particular *gestalt*. This center does indeed have its visible side, for Christ is a man; Mary is a human being; and the Church is human; but its invisibility is more profound, being lost to view in the abysses of God. The believing eye is here and there allowed to catch a deeper glimpse of this center than the outsider, but not even he can begin to sound the full depths of the mystery of the God who has become man.

In the Gospels, alongside the apostles and the seventy disciples, we have the small groups of the Lord's friends, Mary and Martha of Bethany and their brother Lazarus; and apart from these there is also Mary Magdalen, Nicodemus, and others whose existence we see or sense, without getting to know them more closely. These people live very near to the Lord, in the immediacy to him implied by love and self-gift, but we cannot say to what extent they are formed by what we would clearly understand as the "evangelical counsels". Love has its mysteries and keeps silent about them. Genuine love is at home in all the states and forms of life and can never be organized. But Mary of Bethany, who is beloved by the Lord and praised for her contemplative listening to his word, shines out with particular brightness from among this group. She has chosen the one thing necessary, the best part that shall not be taken from her. There is nothing time-conditioned about these words; the emotion and rejoicing come through in Jesus' voice. They justify all those, for all time, who wish to live exclusively and in availability for Jesus, for his word, and for his being, that is, all those who choose the contemplative path, whether in an Order in the usual way or exceptionally in a hermitage, or in a mixture of both, such as we find in the Carthusians and many forms of the life on Athos. As Thérèse of Lisieux has once again shown for our age, a life ordered chiefly to contemplation is a life in the closest proximity to the heart of the Church. The choice of such a life and perseverance in it involve a great renunciation: when it is made out of pure love for God, it is one of the most fruitful things contained in the world of faith. The outside world will no doubt always despise this form of life and feel pity for those who lead it; the veils over their eyes will be all the heavier the less presence the Christian faith has in the public sphere. The classical period, the Middle Ages, even the baroque period made known in various ways their spiritual respect for pure contemplation, despite many abuses in monasteries and many problematic practices on the part of Christians in the world (for example, arranging places in monasteries for younger siblings or widows from noble families, or using the parlors of famous monasteries in the French baroque period for clever religious chatter, and so forth). But abuses always point to a more important, justified use. Against all the activism in the world and in Christianity today, we must absolutely hold fast to the fact—which is one of the most essential aspects of the Church—that nothing can be more welcome or more readily useful to the Lord for the purposes of his salvific providence than the pure gift of self that renounces every calculation and assessment of its own fruits and looks only to him, listens to him, perseveres in availability to him, and finds satisfaction only in him.

3. The Counsels and Human Thinking

In order to make the evangelical counsels comprehensible and intellectually transparent, we have considered them up to this point entirely in the light of the very heart of the Christian mystery; indeed, we have deduced them directly from this heart. This approach would seem to exclude any other way of illuminating them, for if one wanted to justify them from any perspective other than the decisively Christian, the first justification would lose its force to the extent that the second justification became more compelling. But this is only apparently the case, for it is refuted by the general principle that grace does not destroy nature but rather presupposes it and, indeed, perfects it by elevating it (superabundantly). This is why we ought to assume a priori that there must exist a kind of natural basis for the life of the counsels, beginning in drafts, sketches, and attempts within the human sphere something that Christ's word, descending from the wholly other sphere of the divine, exalts and perfects. If this basis did not exist, then the divine word would demand and counsel man to do something impossible and inhuman: We must therefore say at the same time *both* that there are genuine analogies between the Christian and the non-Christian "religious state", monastic or eremitical life, *and* that the ever-greater dissimilarity cuts straight through these analogies. Because of the analogies, and because the Church is a visible religious fellowship, she is genuinely subject in her concrete forms to the science of the sociology of religion that has been developed by Max Weber, Georges Le Bras, W. and H. Goddijn, and others, and that has perhaps found too few adherents as yet. But the sociologist's eye will scarcely be sharp enough to take in the entire dissimilarity (unless he is a Christian and a believer).

The weakest analogy lies in the area of virginity, because outside the Church, the suggestion to renounce marriage is always connected with a denigration of sexuality. This denigration is certainly not justified as such, but if one inquires into its ultimate roots, aspects emerge that are concerned, not directly with the sexual dimension, but with the process of birth and death, the "wheel of coming to be" and passing away (*trokhos tês geneseôs*, Jas 3:6) that strangely enough has forced its way from oriental-Orphic thinking into the Bible. The wise man looks on the cycle of the eternal return of the same (*samsara*) as a fall from which one must escape, no matter how: joy and suffering do not simply balance each other out on this wheel, since suffering outweighs joy by the very fact of the meaninglessness of the ever-circling wheel. The divine cannot ultimately lie within this cycle, even if the divine is a dancing god, who dances all things eternally into being and then dances them back into nothingness. What comes to be and passes away stands out against a background that, compared with both, is nothing, so that nothing can be expected, and nothing has any value. The man of the East, from India via China to Japan, but also the man of Orphism, gnosticism, Neoplatonism and

Sufism, seeks an exit: the non-use of his procreative power is the first condition for attaining the path to God. We see how immensely remote these lines of thought are from biblical revelation, where in the Old Covenant marriage is linked to the promise of future salvation, and in the New Covenant virginity aims at a higher motherhood, whether this is understood bodily in Mary or "eucharistically" in other Christians. The cosmic process can never be understood by the prophets or the New Testament as a meaningless cycle; if such an aspect emerges in the book of Qoheleth, it remains integrated into a much more positive view of the history of the world and of humanity. Sexuality does indeed remain bound to this worldly age that is passing away, "for in the resurrection they neither marry nor are given in marriage, but are like the angels of God in heaven" (Mt 22:30), and the Lord does indeed open up the possibility of a broader, more unlimited love in the unmarried state: but this is not because the flesh and marriage are evil, "for everything created by God is good, and nothing is to be rejected if it is received with thanksgiving" (1 Tim 4:4), but rather because of a participation in the bodily mystery of the Cross and Resurrection.

Stronger analogies can be seen in the area of poverty and the surrender of possessions, analogies with a spirit and a motivation that lead us from the sphere of natural religion to the proximity of the Bible and, in turn, slide back from the Bible through imperceptible transitions into the realm of ethics and sociology. The so-called "communism" of the Church Fathers, for example, of a John Chrysostom, clearly takes its starting point in the charismatic conditions of the primitive Church; and Thomas Aquinas does not at all pose and address the question of the status of private possessions in natural law as we customarily do today: for him, the goods of the earth are in principle the common possession of mankind, and the individual ought to receive what he minimally needs to live, with the obligation of administering whatever he may possess in the spirit of community. The movements in the Middle Ages that sought to live poverty have both a Christian (evangelical) and a natural-sociological foundation: they object to the wealth of the Church, which does not correspond to her essence, but they also know that the poor man in general is closer to God than is the rich man, insofar as he is more strongly dependent on God. Jesus himself said this, and one need not understand each one of his words as a "divine revelation": Jesus can also remind us of the fundamental truths that each man could and should know, if these truths have been lost to view. Moderation is one of the virtues called for in the ethics of all peoples—also in the ethics of the Old Testament, which knows nothing of a vow of poverty. The themes of the fundamental poverty or moderation of the individual and of the fellowship of goods run through the utopias of the modern period, beginning with Thomas More and Campanella; early socialism is inspired by the Sermon on the Mount as much as by economic considerations, and in the background surrounding Marx things are no different. Tolstoy is still another example of the intertwining of natural and Christian motifs. Thus no one will be surprised to find in Asian monasteries a spirit of poverty that, seen from the outside, is closely related to that of Christian communities. Indeed, if one attends to the entire tone of Asiatic religion, it would not be surprising if poverty were understood there even more radically than in Christianity. For where God has not revealed himself and advanced toward man, the normal path to the absolute must consist in separation from all that is relative, temporal, and transient. This detachment from everything that binds and preoccupies the infinite spirit in us is then an aspect of the fundamental religious act itself, and not—as it primarily is in the gospel—an inalienable condition for entry and admission ("Whoever of you does not renounce all that he has cannot be my disciple", Lk 14:33). Outside Christianity, all that man can do with his own activity is to give up the things of the world; nothing positive from God's side awaits him; there is no free act of grace to take hold of him; beyond the action of renunciation lies only the contemplation of that which is non-finite, that is, of the absolute in its unfathomable mystery.[2]

This contemplation brings us to a further important analogy, which clearly does not remain something purely external but also includes an influence of non-Christian forms of life on Christian forms. There can be no doubt that the extreme forms of Eastern monasticism, to which an Evagrius of Pontus and his bountiful school gave an expression as extreme as it is theoretically precise, stand face to face with Indian contemplation. All that is active (renunciation of the world, practice of the virtues)

[2] On this, see the excellent book by Maurus Heinrichs, O.F.M., *Katholische Theologie und asiatisches Denken* (Mainz, 1963).

remains a preliminary stage; the fulfilling act is vision. First comes the *theôria physikê*, which beholds God in the world, through creatures, and then finally the *theôria theologikê*, which beholds God in himself and in his trinitarian light through the mediation of the incarnate Logos. Here what we can call "philosophical" or "natural-religious contemplation" is directly taken up into the Christian act. Another analogous transition takes place from Neoplatonism to Pseudo-Dionysius the Areopagite, the pupil of Proclus; Eckhart's sources, too, are partly philosophical, and influences of Arabic contemplation are either evident or close at hand in Raymon Llull and John of the Cross. The beginnings of such influences are to be seen in the Bible itself, where the wisdom books are illuminated by Stoic and Platonic thought; this is even more true of Philo, whose influence (along with that of gnosticism) on the Alexandrian Fathers and later on Ambrose and Augustine is at work on many levels. If, according to Paul, there exists a natural knowledge of God and man not only can but *must* discern God's eternal power and divinity when he considers the created world (Rom 1:18–20), then there is surely no reason to look with suspicion on Christians continuing to practice religious contemplation: this inheritance is all the more decidedly theirs, since the mystery has been revealed to them in a new and infinitely more radiant way. The gaze of their adoration need now no longer search the space of a mysterious infinite emptiness, for it encounters the mystery of the eternal, gratuitous love in the heart of the absolute; how could this fail to be an adequate goal in life, to adore this mystery that lies at the basis of all that exists?

And if the vicarious character of contemplation has indeed been sensed outside Christianity—it is not a matter of indifference whether there is a monastery in a Chinese landscape, whether monks pray on behalf of a kingdom, or whether the emperor can consult them in important questions—then this character stands out in a far brighter light in the religion of the Cross and of the Eucharist. It is foolish and evidence of intellectual limitation to look down on every existential act of genuine philosophy and dismiss it as irrelevant in the name of biblical revelation. For this act, in which the human spirit questions being in its mode of being, is the fundamental act and the characteristic dignity of the spirit and, thus, of man in the natural cosmos. All technical activity remains indifferent and in a twilight state until this fundamental act has bestowed on it its place and orientation in the hierarchy of values. The philosophical act and the religious (or mystical, if you will) act are fundamentally one and the same. And the Christian, too, cannot admire enough mankind's existential commitment to this act, as it seeks after its form in non-Christian religions, in monasteries and religious communities.

The analogy of obedience would be the most difficult to determine. It exists, of course; obedience holds sway in all relationships between superiors and inferiors, in the family, state, society, economics, technology, the military, and so forth. This natural obedience is in part ethically and even religiously motivated, and in this respect it is enjoined by the Bible (Paul says that children must obey their parents, wives their husbands, slaves their masters, subjects the state; and in each case the one who gives orders represents something of the divine authority: Eph 5; Col 3; Rom 13; 1 Pet 2–3, and so on), sometimes with an explicit reference to the example of Christ, above all with regard to the humble attitude of obedience, sometimes also with a reference to the humility required on the part of the one who commands. Natural obedience is already an utterly mysterious and risky act, full of promise and threat, potential blessing and disaster, since it involves the venture of trustingly surrendering power and oversight over oneself to the one who issues commands. This surrender can be abused by him in many ways, and in the one who obeys, it must be decided whether it springs from courage (to entrust oneself) or cowardice (seeking to pass responsibility onto another). Where obedience enters the specifically religious sphere and is meant to be the expression of the fundamental act of the person, it is essential to have a guarantee of religious competence in the one giving orders. This is how it was in the beginnings of Christian monasticism: the "fathers" to whom a learner entrusted himself were proven men of the Spirit who had received the divine gifts of wisdom and also the gifts of religious-pedagogical guidance. Here we see at once the analogy to the oriental forms of community: the pupil entrusts himself to a well-known teacher (*swâmi*) of proven knowledge and ability and lets this man introduce him into the world of religion, exercise oversight over his ascetic steps and practices, and lead him to contemplation; in some cases he spends his whole life as his disciple. This relationship is altered in many ways within Christianity, but not in such a way as to destroy the formal similarities. For, here (1) the Master who gives commands is himself the first to obey, taking the disciple into his own obedient following of the Father's will. (2) Through his obedience to God the Father, the obedient Master opens up a revelatory insight into the depths of the triune God of love, where it is the eternal attitude of love on the part of the Son that gives eternal expression to the fontal mystery of the Father through utter transparency and selflessness: as the Word of the Father. (3) The Master's act of obedience is not only a pedagogical model for the disciple but, in its self-renouncing love, is the absolute soteriological act: obedience not only educates, it also redeems. (4) The Master founds his Church and gives her his own Holy Spirit, so that alongside the personal charisms there is also an objective charismatic dimension of the Church. It is indeed desirable and imperative that both forms of charism coincide in a spiritual father (abbot, superior), since each calls for the other and they promote and elevate each other; but one must reckon in the Catholic realm with a tension between the two forms, a tension that is not without its benefits, since it keeps the disciple from becoming too one-sidedly attached to a single personality, helping him to see more the office than the person, more the authority of Christ and of God than a personal authority—and this remains the meaning and the goal of every religious obedience. Although these four differences between Christian and non-Christian religious obedience remain quite clear, they must not lead us to throw every similarity overboard, especially since (as we have shown) the Bible sanctions ordinary forms of human obedience and fills them with a Christian meaning.

All the analogies between a Christian and a non-Christian life in poverty, virginity, contemplation, and obedience are fundamentally important for insight into the essence both of general human religiosity and of the distinctively Christian life of faith. They are evidence that the Christian life of the counsels goes farther along a path on which humanity as a whole has walked from the very beginning—with other intentions, perhaps, but to the extent that these efforts are searching for God, they do not lie totally remote from the Christian truth. Human efforts always remain uncertain and preliminary: "They seek God, in the hope that they might feel after him and find him. Yet he is not far from each one of us" (Acts 17:27). From the outside, there is no way to discern the extent to which the silent God in the silence of his mystery wishes to make himself known to those who grope toward him. From a Christian perspective, it is altogether impossible. For many graces exist even outside the sphere of the visible Church, graces that are determined by the world's Redeemer alone and are taken away from Peter's official competence ("If it is my will that he [the representative of pure love] remain until I come, what is that to you?", Jn 21:22). It is perhaps easier to tell where the windows remain shut, indeed, are shut specifically by religious practices, than to tell where they open. They are closed wherever man imagines that he is something because of the "virtue" of his poverty, celibacy, contemplation, and his obedience and becomes puffed up in spiritual arrogance; but this often happens to Christians, too, and we cannot formulate a rule saying it must always be the case outside Christianity. It is entirely possible for one who has done all that is humanly possible (facienti quod est in se non negatur gratia) to remain standing with humble perseverance before the threshold of the silent mystery of God, hoping that a few crumbs for the little dogs may fall from the master's table. "O woman," said Jesus to the Gentile woman, "great is your faith! Be it done for you as you desire" (Mt 15:27–28).

4. The Situation Today

We began with an analysis of the contemporary situation in its harsh polarization: unsparing criticism, on the one hand, of the traditional forms of the state of the counsels, which are rejected in general terms as not having their source in the Gospels, as "Constantinian" and, hence, superseded or at least in need of large-scale revision today—and, on the other hand, undisturbed by this, a fresh kindling of the ancient fire, for example, through Thérèse of Lisieux or Charles de Foucauld and everything that has blossomed anew in their wake. The second chapter, which showed the New Testament foundation for the life of the counsels, provided a basic response to many of the initial objections, but probably did not lay to rest the final anxiety about the concrete forms that have developed over the course of history and still exist today. However that may be, we cannot allow ourselves to forget that there is no form of life within a mysterious structure like the Church of Christ that can be exhaustively understood and, therefore, none that could be organized in a way that would be ultimately satisfactory to men; the Church does possess a visibility, as community and as individual member, but she is no *societas perfecta* comparable to the state, since the inner aspect of her mysteries (for example, of the sacraments and their effects) is inaccessible to men and something they can never get under their control. Thus a form of life that is founded primarily on the invisible—the invisible aspect of faith, of the efficacy of what man institutes, of the promise of a "hundredfold"—can never satisfy the psychologist and sociologist, who are concerned with mental health and with what helps human life. This makes us cautious, not to say suspicious, vis-à-vis the "progressive" Christians who call so loudly for reform in the state of the counsels; for if one looks more closely, one sees that they make wholesale judgments about things they know only by hearsay or that they generalize on the basis of tragic individual cases. Or else the values on which the life of the counsels is very consciously based are compared with other values that are foreign to it, and this comparison decides a priori against the life of the counsels. Thus, for example, we are told that one who vows obedience is necessarily and essentially "immature", but that today is the time when humanity is finally coming into its own and becoming "mature", and so on. This implies that the one who obeys has replaced his own conscience with an external norm, so that he is no longer capable of grasping the inner summons of a situation as it presents itself: what is most important passes right by him, and he is therefore never capable of exercising a genuine influence on his age. We are told that it is more challenging and harder to give a response appropriate to the specific situation than to measure it against an alien criterion. We have already heard the corresponding objections to virginity and have seen how they may be refuted. The same is true of contemplation, which is often portrayed as an obsolete luxury. As for poverty, it is precisely the non-Christian motivations and movements sketched above that can give pause to the one who seeks to condemn.

The advantage of the various criticisms of all traditional forms is that any form that wishes to remain in existence must rethink itself from the ground up and must replenish itself from the original source. This process—which occurs in so many different ways it defies classification—is one characteristic of the Church today. Extremes come starkly to the fore here: on the one hand, the need to accompany our age, to make Christians present in today's de-Christianized society, is embraced with full seriousness; and, on the other, the supernatural requirements of Christ's salvific work are embraced with full seriousness, to make oneself totally available to his needs for love, for sacrifice, for contemplation. This is why the paths and solutions we have considered stand in a new internal dynamic, one that produces certain relatively new forms of the life of the counsels: namely, the so-called secular institutes.

Essential structural changes can scarcely be expected from the great active Orders of the modern period, the Dominicans and Jesuits, with the clear hierarchical organization that encompasses the whole of their life. Moreover, they possess so much internal flexibility that we can expect individual personalities within them to give rise to new impulses in the present age and in the Church, pointing the way for others: powerful thinkers like Sertillanges, Congar, Chenu, de Lubac, Teilhard de Chardin, Karl Rahner, and very many others. The great Franciscan family has its greatest potential precisely in what is often seen as its weakness or danger: Francis was a charismatic who distanced himself from every kind of binding organization, for he understood only too well that Christianity can never find anything more than a gradual, analogous realization in mankind, that its authentic reality lies where only a very few can reach it (on Alverna), and that it can remain alive only in the open dynamism of love between the supreme wealth of grace in heaven and the supreme poverty with the crucified Lord and his poorest brothers on earth. This unprotected openness ought to allow the Franciscan charism today to arrive at wholly new, surprising, and compelling forms. At the moment, it is the oldest tree of Western monasticism that is showing forth new life out of its criss-crossing branches, proof that, no more than the Church herself are the great Orders bound by the law of history: to grow, to blossom, and to fade. A new, radical monasticism, indeed an eremitical movement, has spread out from France and taken hold of England, Italy, and continents across the sea; Dom Jean Leclercq has made himself its theological and literary spokesman. There exists a decided effort in the whole Benedictine Order to abolish the cleft between priestly, educated choir monks and less educated lay brothers, who hitherto carried out only subordinate services and were not admitted to prayer in choir: on the one hand, by restricting the number of monks who are candidates for the priesthood to the minimum necessary—the monks as a rule seek to be laymen—and, on the other hand, by elevating the status of the lay brothers. Many monasteries are opening their doors to the world in order to make it possible for laymen in the world, for example, academics in professional life, to participate in the religious life for a few months: *Kloster auf Zeit* (temporary religious life). Other monasteries take the opposite path and strive to increase their own contact with the world, not only by participating in pastoral work in the surrounding parishes, which has been customary for a long time in many places, but also by decentralizing the big abbeys and breaking them up into small communities that are to live in the midst of the world. This movement touches the boundary, so to speak, of the "right wing" of the secular institutes, which we will discuss in a moment. But this development can also occur when the Orders that are "closed" in the old sense seek to extend themselves outside their own walls through a secular institute that lives according to their own essential religious spirit. Thus a Benedictine abbey in the Rhineland has a secular institute fashioned in its spirit in the Rhineland's big cities; the Dominican friars of Walberberg have a "Dominican community of women" with members scattered across Germany; Carmel has an international secular institute called Notre Dame de Vie, and there are many secular institutes inspired by Ignatius and under Jesuit guidance.

In all these movements, we see a rhythmic pendulum swing between the internal and the external, Church and world, hiddenness and public character, contemplation and action. Today, at the center point of this pendulum swing, explicitly embracing both extremes, stand the secular institutes, which were solemnly recognized by Pius XII in 1947 as a new ecclesial form of life and were incorporated into universal canon law with a law of their own. The idea that unites the tremendous variety of these institutes is to join the evangelical counsels together with the life of an ordinary Christian in the world and in a secular job. Naturally, such a union cannot take place in a merely external manner; it must lead to an organic interpenetration of both standpoints and their spiritual and intellectual demands, which has in fact led to a rethinking of the "Constantinian" forms of religious life as a whole. For what has been considered since Anthony the Great to be the foundation of the entire life of the counsels, that is, departure from the world (as a literal leaving of everything, including the abandonment of wife and child and the renunciation of self-determination), is here called into question, and appeal is made to the Gospels, in order to discern Jesus' genuine intention. He certainly did not primarily intend a literal *anakhôrêsis* ("withdrawal"), since the desert, too, is "world"—and more than anything else it is the sinful man who goes to live in the desert. No doubt is possible about the "diacritical point" of remaining unmarried; nor is doubt possible about its positive fundamental Christian meaning: freedom for a more general love, in the universality of the Cross, the Eucharist, and the omnipresent risen humanity of Jesus: freedom for the agape that is celebrated between Christ the Bridegroom and the Church-Bride as representative of all mankind. If this is the center, then the renunciation of earthly possessions can be understood to mean that the one who forgoes them uses earthly goods in the detachment and selflessness required by his Christian mission in the Church and the world. For himself, he leads a poor and moderate life; for others, according to his possibilities, he is generous, an example of how to deal with money and goods in the spirit of the gospel. The real difficulty seems to lie in the field of obedience. One can blow these difficulties up casuistically and dramatize them as a perplexing flood of questions, but in reality they are no more serious than in the case of every genuine Christian who must achieve a harmony in every situation between the demands of the secular constellation and the command of his Christian conscience (and that means, in concrete terms, what Mother Church feels and believes and counsels or orders in these particular circumstances). Only the superficiality or dullness that one often finds in Christian consciences imagines that it already knows all the answers and thus fails to see that there is a constant call for a new synthesis. Nor is obedience weakened or reduced in any way in a secular institute—provided that it is exercised properly, both by the superior and by the one who stands under him. In ecclesial obedience (since the superior can represent only the Church and her spirit) the subject accepts a task in a secular field. He is "sent" into this field and must cultivate it in the free and mature responsibility demanded by every such field of work, with the professional knowledge it requires (and which the superior normally does not have), knowledge for which no obedience, no external authority can be a substitute. And yet this is a freedom and a maturity that stem from obedience, from existence in the state of mission, and that are thus at least as close to the archetypal existence of Jesus in his mission as the more literal obedience that can be exercised meaningfully only behind monastery walls. Many intermediary stages are possible between this literal obedience, which renounces all initiatives of one's own —an unheard-of ascetic penitential practice—and obedience in a secular institute: thus, obedience in an active priestly and educational Order is already much closer to the second pole, because here and in similar cases the individual is always given responsibility of his own and left to exercise it. Nevertheless, it is easier to be recalled from any given task undertaken as a service inside the Church than in the case where a secular profession has been assumed, perhaps after a necessary training lasting years or decades; the outcome of this education, namely, the exercise of one's professional work, is analogous to the spiritual professional work of the priest, from which no bishop can or will ever recall him. Most importantly for the relationship of obedience, which holds even in the mature responsibility exercised in professional work or elsewhere, it will be necessary to keep alive the original zeal, the freshness of sacrifice, of prayer, of faith, and of love. This relationship of obedience will preserve the person from the inevitable tendency to self-deceptions and will be like a trellis that binds up a plant pulling constantly downward, so that the person grows in the direction of God, which will always be at the same time the direction of the Cross. Where this obedience is grasped and lived in a vital way, it can be understood less and less literally and more and more spiritually; but precisely the spiritual man has a need, even a yearning, to feel the hardness of the wood of the Cross on occasion, to reassure himself that he is in contact with it. He prizes the humiliation before which the earthly man shrinks back, for he loves to be able to prove to the Lord and the Church that he is still ready, at any price, to renounce his own will.

It is thus clear that nothing prevents one from living out the substance of the evangelical counsels even in a secular profession and environment. They come together more than ever here to form a single, simple act, to which the new communities prefer to give the same name we used at the beginning of this essay, the name suggested by the papal documents: the consecration of the whole of one's life to God (*consecratio vitæ*). A consecration understood in this way leaves much room for different concrete forms, and the communities in fact can and should work out the desired synthesis themselves in an original way, avoiding an external dependence on the forms of the old Orders. Rather, as Pius XII says, the "secular element" in these communities, "which forms the entire justification of their existence, should find expression in all things". If nothing may be taken away from the evangelical counsels in the sense of a compromise, this new reality must nevertheless be brought into existence "in the midst of the world", indeed as "coming out of the world [in sæculo, veluti ex sæculo]".[3] Of course, since the practical relationship to the "world" in the Orders and old congregations could and should take a variety of forms, depending on whether and to what extent they are purely contemplative or active-contemplative, the new formula, too, can be applied in quite various ways. We have already

[3] J. Beyer, *Die kirchlichen Urkunden für die Weltgemeinschaften*, Der neue Weg, vol. 1, Schriftenreihe für Weltgemeinschaften (Einsiedeln: Johannes Verlag, 1963), 46.

mentioned a "right wing" where the secular institutes directly touch the forms of the Orders and congregations, with a strong emphasis on life in common, Mass in common (in a house chapel of their own), perhaps even some Hours of the monastic Office (as in the Venio House in Munich, which deliberately follows a Benedictine orientation), without detriment to the secular professional work of the individual members, as well as the obligation of periodic interruption of professional life for months or perhaps a whole year in meditative retreat (for example, in the Carmelite community mentioned above), an understanding of poverty and obedience with a very strong analogy to already existing forms of religious life. An extreme "left wing" emphasizes above all "secularity": the members normally live scattered, either in their families or alone in a working-class milieu; they have no kind of novitiate period that would separate them from others, but are instructed and informed about other members of the community only through circular letters; they meet the others (as in Caritas Christi, founded by Father Perrins, O.P.) once a year for a few days of retreat and holiday; poverty and obedience here are primarily a "spirit"; government is in the hands of a "community council" rather than a "superior"; and the profession and one's involvement in it determine almost entirely the matter and form of the Christian decisions. Between these two wings lies a movable center, with many nuances. Another area, which is related but not completely identical, in which the institutes adopt different positions concerns the question of the extent to which the constellations of worldly power may and should be brought into play in the service of the kingdom of God. At the one end stand the numerous groups we mentioned that are founded in the spirit of Charles de Foucauld, and next to these we could place the movement of the Focolarini (neither of these are primarily secular institutes, but they have a potential to produce such institutes): they insist above all on the distinctly Christian element, the disinterested love that seeks no profit, no earnings, no success. At the other end we find movements that make every possible effort to obtain key political, economic, and intellectual positions for themselves (government posts, university professorships, banks, newspapers and magazines, publishing houses, student houses, indeed entire universities of their own), as above all in the case of Opus Dei, which, having many members, began in Spain and clearly bears an inner relationship to Franco's ideology.[4] But such undertakings remain a minority and do not determine the general characteristic spirit of the new secular institutes. Most of these are not externally disguised but are marked internally by the spirit of anonymity; they do not consciously seek power or even measurable apostolic successes, but content themselves with the testimony of Christian "presence" (*présence*), above all in de-Christianized milieux. This is especially the case with the French "shock troops" who take up the most difficult and thankless social tasks with the courage of the early Christians and have largely taken the place of the worker priests (Le Nid, L'Équipe apostolique dans le sous-prolétariat, Les Petits Frères des

[4] Since this article was written, Opus Dei has left the ranks of the secular institutes.

Pauvres, the group led by Father Loew, O.P., in Marseilles, and many others). We do not yet see many such pioneering groups in the German-speaking lands.[5]

The secular institutes of the present day are mostly small vessels on the waves of the high seas, left to their own seeking and their own experiences; if they prove themselves, they will be recognized, but if not, they will fall into crisis and sink. Of the numerous applications for approbation in Rome (about two hundred), only a few—and perhaps not always the most interesting and most appropriate for the age—have been definitively recognized. But since it was the Church herself that propagated this new formula, she has opened up a wide field for experimentation, where many new things will be tried in practice and also wholly unexpected theological decisions will be made.

The most important of these theological decisions is a certain relativization and leveling out of the ecclesial "states of life", which since the Middle Ages have often shut each other out in a virtually caste-like way. Strictly speaking, since the members of secular institutes belong neither to the "religious" nor to the "laity" as they are defined in canon law, they participate in both forms of life, or rather, in their return to the basic New Testament rock, they have opened up a place wherein the distinction between the religious and those in the world has not yet been made. Karl Rahner's attempt to situate the mem-

[5] H. A. Timmermann gives an overview of secular institutes in the German-speaking countries, with a comprehensive bibliography, in *Weltgemeinschaften im deutschen Sprachraum*, Der neue Weg, vol. 2 (Einsiedeln: Johannes Verlag, 1963) (now out of print).

bers of the ecclesiastical hierarchy together with all religious and members of secular institutes under the common designation of "clergy", as distinct from genuine (*de jure* married) lay people in the world, remains artificial and cannot be justified theologically.

The more profoundly Christian approach, by contrast, would be to try to view the entire Christian existence—prior to all distinctions between states of life—as a unity. For every Christian (as Romans 6 says) has died to the old world with Christ in baptism and has been given citizenship in a new, heavenly world (which for the old world is something still to come), so that all are in this sense "aliens and pilgrims" here below (1 Pet 2:11), those who live and work in the world no less than priests and religious. But all are called, from this standpoint, to collaborate with Christ in the redemption of the world, each in his own way. All have promised the Lord fidelity for the whole of their lives in baptism, and this baptismal vow is the foundation of every Christian existence, including the vowed existence in the state of the counsels, which was correctly interpreted in the Middle Ages as a "second baptism"; this naturally does not mean that the first baptism was too weak or is even repeatable in any sense, but rather that the vow of baptism should henceforth be sounded out existentially and in its depths. But it is impossible in principle to be more or less dead to the world, just as it is impossible in principle to be more or less turned to the world in the love of Christ. Neither turning away from the world nor turning to the world is a Christian category, especially if they are applied individually or played off against each other or distributed among different groups of Christians. Believers are sealed with a single consecration, in imitation of Christ's own consecration for the entire world (Jn 17:19), and each one receives his own charism within this same consecration (1 Cor 7:7).

Since there also exist secular institutes for (secular) priests and since the same community can contain clerical and lay members, the boundary between clergy and laity is also softened and leveled out according to circumstances. Moreover, many institutes count married people among their members in a wider sense; the existential connection between these persons and those who live in the counsels is essentially much closer than for example between a First or Second Order of the old observance and the so-called "Third Orders" and "oblates", who share in the spirituality of the Order only outside the monastery walls and in a much weakened form. Thus we can await a very fruitful and happy integration of ecclesial life in the Catholic Church from the new communities. What is coming to life here is the Church herself, not only as a sociological "people of God" or as the somewhat unfortunate organological structure of a *Corpus Mysticum*, but as that representation of the humanity formed and redeemed by God which is to become the spouse of the Lamb in the end time: answering, in the love of the obedient bride (Zion–Mary–Ecclesia), with the unconditional consecration of the words "Let your will be done", "Be it done to me according to your word."

III.

THE EVANGELICAL COUNSELS IN TODAY'S WORLD?

1. The Urgency of the Question

Christianity today is threatened at the most profound level—less by persecutions (though these, too, occur) than by the ever-increasing difficulty of bridging the gap between Christ's message and demands, on the one hand, and the modern world's ideals and presuppositions, on the other. The humanism that drew upon classical antiquity had a long tradition of contact with the gospel. But technological civilization goes on its way without any concern for philosophy and religion; the one who wishes to come along must "leave everything" and "follow" it, for otherwise he will remain a romantic who fails to keep up with the times; he will lose his connection and perish. We also see a great many theologians today feverishly engaged in "demythologizing" the Bible, that is, liberating it from all the "dead weight" that modern man finds alien, "unbearable", undesirable, and inassimilable, as he marches into the future. What is left is often not much more than the light luggage of a social humanism; love of neighbor is the measure and criterion of the love of God; prayer—especially contemplative prayer (which belongs to a past contemplative-philosophical world view)—is to be replaced by active involvement, which is prayer enough;

the passivity of undergoing suffering (a religion of the Cross) is to be transformed into a courageous struggle against humanity's suffering in all its forms; the ideal of obedience can at most be a preliminary stage on the way to a Christian-human maturity, responsibility, and competence; the ideal of poverty yields ground to the socialistic ideal of common possession; the ideal of virginity is seen as closely linked to the imminent expectation of the end of the world (so that there would be no more time to marry), but perhaps also to a certain gnostic suspicion of the sexual sphere; not only have we gotten over these, so that we are only now beginning to construct a genuine theology of marriage, but it is only with the evolutionary picture of the world that we have attained a fundamental sense of what the human future means, so that care for "what is to come" (the procreation of children) has even become a Christian-human obligation. This shows us how deeply today's "investigation of world views" is an attack on the fundamental views of the Bible. For it must be the case that if Christ was a man of his time, then he must have thought, lived, and expressed himself in the time-conditioned ideas of the contemporary world view; these ideas are no longer valid for us, and some of them have been replaced by contrary ideas. For the Jews of late antiquity, the present world was at its end, and their apocalyptic vision awaited from God the irruption of a new condition of the world. For the Greeks, who are always Platonists in some respect, the soul has been banished from heaven, falling to the earth through sin: it is a "stranger" here below, and its ethical-religious striving requires it to find its way back from this world to the other world, from earth to heaven. Our world view today appears diametrically opposed to both conceptions: in the evolutionary world view, we have still endless time ahead of us until the Omega Day, so that all the practical preparations for a speedy return of Christ ("Watch and pray") become obsolete. Moreover, in this new vision of the world, man comes essentially from below, from nature: he is no stranger, but one who is completely at home in the world, and his ethic will consist in remaining "faithful" to the world in the deepest way.

Such perspectives are very popular today, and if one follows them faithfully to their logical conclusions along the lines sketched above, nothing more of Christianity will survive than a humanism colored by the Enlightenment, with a few reminiscences from the Sermon on the Mount. But one who looks on the Bible as the Word of God will follow the methods of demythologization with the greatest distrust, because they implicitly elevate "modern man" as the criterion for determining what is true and false, what is relevant and superseded in the Bible, thus allowing one to throw onto the scrap heap whatever does not "suit" him or "correspond" to him in an obvious way. If the Bible is the Word of God, however, then nothing essential in it can be obsolete; or, to put this more precisely, even in the *garment* of a natural, unscientific world view, which can in a certain sense be complemented or corrected by science, it is possible to express *contents* that are independent of any relative and historical world view. "Heaven and earth will pass away, but my words will not pass away."

One who sits in judgment on the Bible merely on the

basis of the "investigation into world views" will have lost all possibility of hearing God's Word in it. But anyone who allows himself to be struck in the core of his being by this Word will be confronted, today no less than in the past, with decisions affecting his life. The fundamental question remains the same: Is it true that Christ is the Son of God and that he died for my sins, so that, if I may have access to the God of love and of salvation, it is through his gift? Is he my *auctor vitæ* (author of life) (Acts 4:15)? If this is true, then this fact is the foundation of my life, and it cannot be relativized by any evolution, any fidelity to the world. And yet, at the same time, "something has happened" to humanity, and the Christian must involve himself in the decisions of his contemporaries, both because of solidarity with his brothers and because of his Christian commission. How can these be brought into unity? The answer is best given from the place where the Christian form of life comes most *radically* into view today: totally consecrated to Christ, totally present in today's world. This is the form of life of today's "secular institutes", which do not in the least indicate the path *all* Christians must take but which certainly constitute a *model* that permits us to discern what Christian involvement in this time means. The Holy Spirit has always helped the Church in times of crisis through a new model of evangelical discipleship: Benedict, Francis, and Ignatius have supplied such models. Nor is this denied to our own age. We can address this issue only in general outlines here. But since the essence and the validity of the so-called evangelical counsels are called into question today more profoundly than ever, we must begin by demonstrating that they are anchored in the supra-temporal core and heart of Christ's revelation.

2. *Biblical Foundations*

The foundation of a life according to the counsels of Jesus Christ is *loving gratitude* for what he has done for me. Naturally, this love presupposes the faith that his life and suffering have freed me from my guilt and opened up for me access to God, the access of a child to his Father. He has redeemed me at the price of his being utterly stripped and robbed of all his bodily and spiritual possessions: How could I show that I acknowledge this in any other way than by at least offering him everything that belongs to me? If it is in all seriousness true (as my faith tells me) that I am allowed to live in the light of God because another *human being* descended for me into the darkness of my sin and my distance from God and suffered these vicariously down to their very foundations,[1] how then could I repose calmly in my light, without continuously thinking of the dark Brother in whose flesh and blood I am rooted? This is why Paul "decided to know nothing among you except Jesus Christ and him crucified" (1 Cor 2:2), for if "one has died for all, therefore all have died . . . that they might live no longer for themselves but for him who for their sake died and was raised" (2 Cor 5:14–15). It is for this reason that Paul has "died" to the world, "that I might live to God. I have been crucified with Christ; it is no

[1] One should read again Schiller's *Bürgschaft*, which contains the verse: "Now he is nailed to the Cross."

longer I who live, but Christ who lives in me; and the life I now live in the flesh I live by faith in the Son of God, who loved me and gave himself for me" (Gal 2:19–20).

But Christ's *total gift of self*, through which I am redeemed and have become a child of God, is delineated precisely through the sphere of the "evangelical counsels": "For you know the grace of our Lord Jesus Christ, that though he was rich, yet for your sake he became poor, so that by his poverty you might become rich" (2 Cor 8:9). And "though he was in the form of God, he did not count equality with God a thing to be grasped, but emptied himself, taking the form of a servant, being born in the likeness of men. And being found in human form he humbled himself and became obedient unto death, even death on a cross" (Phil 2:6–8; cf. Heb 5:8–9). And in order to make his human nature the pure instrument of the redemption of all, letting himself be exhibited as last of all, like a man sentenced to death . . . the refuse of the world, the offscouring of all things" (1 Cor 4:9, 13), and to become, thanks to this total and exhaustive exploitation, the eucharistic flesh and blood that is distributed ad infinitum, he remained virginal. For it is almost inconceivable to think that a body that once belonged to a particular woman could now also be the body that wishes to belong *totally* to every individual in the sacrament. His fruitfulness in its totality enters his Church and, through her, enters mankind.

Christ's life in poverty, obedience, and virginity is not only the expression of divine love for us, but it is the effective, indeed the only effective, means of our redemption. Only because he has totally dispossessed himself of all that belongs to him as God can he load our sins into his own emptiness; only because he is totally obedient to the Father can he "let himself be led where he does not wish to go" (Jn 21:18; Mt 26:39), into the night of our guilt where he is abandoned by God; only because he is virginal is his gift of himself in the flesh not bound to the limited temporal succession of human generations but is free to accomplish salvation supratemporally for the whole world ("holy" means: completely consecrated "in body and soul", 1 Cor 7:34). Thus the "one thing necessary" is accomplished by the love that renounces everything. It is through this love—not through speeches, actions, organizations, and *aggiornamenti*—that the world was redeemed. And since Christ has given us everything that is his, he also gives to those who belong to him the form of his own life. He does not do so at a subsequent stage, but from the very outset, insofar as he wishes his Mother to be a virgin and can make use of her only as such and insofar as he begins his apostolic life at once by taking men into his own act of leaving all things (Mt 8:19f.) and into his own total obedience (Mt 8:22; 9:9, and so forth). The apostles' surrender of all they have is thus not in the first place a way they themselves have chosen to express their gratitude but is itself obedience (Mt 19:27; the same is true of Paul: Acts 9:6). "I want obedience, not sacrifices" (1 Sam 15:22; Ps 40:7–9; Heb 10:5–8), since sacrifices are limited and self-chosen offerings, which express only their own religious will, whereas obedience is the fundamentally unlimited readiness out of which God himself can draw the fruit he needs for his salvific work. But just as Christ was not allowed during his lifetime to harvest what he sowed through his renunciation, or even to get a complete overview of it, so one who follows Christ cannot demand to see what fruit he is bearing for the kingdom of God.

Christ's attitude is the *fulfillment of the Old Covenant.* Abraham was called by God to be the ancestor of the people of faith, and his faith at its roots was an obedience without understanding (departure from his native land, the sacrifice of Isaac). All Israel must live in this obedience, which is dependent on God's continually free disposal—and it is impossible to know what he will come to demand tomorrow (for example, through a prophet). But this kind of total dependence on God is at the same time poverty, as emerges with ever greater clarity in Israel until from the prophets onward the term "the poor of Yahweh" (those without possessions, those deprived of their rights, those reduced to servitude by the rich) becomes the real name for those who are loyal to the faith; the first words of the Sermon on the Mount, "Blessed are the poor in spirit", thus have a place to start from. And although Israel must also be a people of the flesh, procreating children in the hope of the Messiah, God already lays claim to the sexual sphere, too, through the sign of circumcision. Its fundamental meaning is to be the pure expression of faith's hope (Tob 3:18; 8:3–9), but this meaning is fulfilled only with the coming of Christ. *After* him, marriage will still be able to be a "great mystery" only to the extent that it is an image in the sexual sphere of the suprasexual (eucharistic) bodily relationship between Christ the Bridegroom and the Church his Bride

(Eph 5:25–33). Thus the "evangelical counsels" are not a "secondary shoot" in the New Covenant but are the completion of the main trunk of the history of faith.

This is also why *the Church* of the New Covenant is herself a product of the total gift of self, or of the life of the counsels. On earth, she is "built upon the foundation of the apostles and [New Testament] prophets, Christ Jesus himself being the corner-stone" (Eph 2:20), and she retains this structure even in heaven (Rev 21:14); indeed, following the archetype of Mary, she must be entirely a "pure virgin betrothed to Christ" (2 Cor 11:2), "without spot or wrinkle". One can say that there is nothing "institutional" in the Church that is not, as it were, "covered" by the gold reserves of the existentially lived gift of self. Thus, the Eucharist is the lived gift of the Lord's self into death; confession is the absolution of sins brought about on the Cross in the pains of death, while baptism is the believer's imitation of Christ that shares in his death and burial, so that the believer, too, is "dead to sin, once for all" (Rom 6:3–12). For every *opus operatum* has truly been accomplished by someone, namely, by Christ, who draws into his work those who through their total gift of self belong to the realm of the roots of the Church.[2] The Church as an institution belongs thus to the post-Easter sphere (and this doubtless means that the formulation in Matthew 16:18–19 belongs there, too); in the

[2] The chief goal of St. Ignatius' Spiritual Exercises is to lead men into this radical sphere where the Church is, as it were, only beginning to emerge out of Christ's deeds, the sphere of those who hear his call to follow him and "offer their whole person for this work" (Spiritual Exercises, no. 96).

"good news" about Jesus' earthly life, everything is still existential, and what Jesus wants in his proclamation of the kingdom of God is to establish lives that can then become "pillars in his Church" (Gal 2:9; Rev 3:12). Thus it is logical that the spirit of the life of the counsels should permeate the entire life of the Church, rising up from the roots; even when Christians have possessions, determine themselves, and marry, they must do so in the spirit of self-renouncing love: they must possess as if they had no possessions, dispose as if only God were disposing, be married as though they were not married (1 Cor 7:29–31). Paul explains this principle very clearly: The point is not that married people should make no use of their marriage—indeed, this is expressly forbidden them. Thus the meaning can only be that the "model" of their love must be the perfect selflessness of Jesus' gift of himself to his Church, his perfect willingness to bear all things, and his Church's perfect devotion to him (Eph 5:25ff.).

The original obedience in the biblical sense is a total readiness to follow the directive of the free God who speaks through an angel or a man (Moses, the prophets, Christ) and leaves no room for "ifs" or "buts". The apostles left everything in literal obedience to Christ, in whom they as yet saw only a *man* filled with the Spirit of God. (It was only with the Resurrection that they received insight into the genuine divinity of Christ.) Paul demands a very close obedience from his communities—just as he himself follows Christ and the Holy Spirit—and brooks no contradiction. He demands (for example, in 2 Corinthians) the same kind of "obedience of the understanding" ("We take every thought captive to obey Christ", 2 Cor 10:5) that was earlier lived out by Abraham, Moses, Job, and above all Christ on the Mount of Olives; this kind of obedience is genuinely embodied in the Church now only in the life of the counsels.

3. A Few Consequences

This tightly compressed overview of what revelation says allows us to draw a few consequences.

1. What counts for the Bible is man's total gift of self to God, the total "Yes, Father" (Mt 11:26), "thy will!" (Lk 22:42; Mk 6:10), "handmaid of the Lord!" (Lk 1:38). This is faith and love. Insofar as God's call demands it, this is the love that is subsequently articulated into the three areas of poverty, obedience, and virginity. There exists only *one* vowing of oneself, one vow (with three areas) that makes no exceptions but is available in such a way that God can dispose over everything. Such an offer can ultimately not be limited in a temporal sense ("temporary vows" exist at most during a time of probation; but such vows no more exist than "temporary marriage" can exist). The entire Christian power of self-gift lies in the commitment for the whole of one's life.

One who gives himself in this way to God wants to do and be *what God needs*. Man cannot do anything more; this is why "perfection" lies in this gift.[3] Thus such a man

[3] Many take offense at the term "state of perfection"; to meet their concerns, one speaks of a *status perfectionis acquirendæ*, not *acquisitæ*. This is of course correct, since every man must fight against his failings to the end, and his own perfection always lies ahead of him. Paul says precisely this at Philippians 3:12–14. Nevertheless, he says in the

does not speculate about what the outcome will be for himself. He does not speculate (a) about whether what is demanded is easier or harder than the life of an ordinary married Christian (in one respect it is easier, because he stands "undivided" in the service of the Lord, whereas others are "divided" and have "anxiety" [1 Cor 7:26, 34]; in another respect it is harder, because one must renounce so much, and this is why it is not "something for everyone" [1 Cor 7:9; cf. Lk 8:38f.]). He does not speculate (b) whether his personality will develop harmoniously here or perhaps suffer disadvantage (on the one hand, he wants to give himself, to make sacrifices, to cease to develop; on the other hand, the Lord guarantees him a hundredfold already in this life, though not without the Cross: Mk 10:30). He does not speculate (c) whether this gift of self is "modern" or not (it will *never* be modern, since the total Christian act of faith will never be anything

---

next verse (3:15), "Let those of us who are perfect be thus minded"—in the sense that a man who sincerely makes available to God all that he has can do absolutely nothing better. For such a one is not aiming at his own perfection, since "love does not seek that which is its own" (1 Cor 13:5). No one enters a monastery for his own sake (in order to attain his own "perfection"); such an act is meaningful only for the sake of God and of men, as a contribution to Christ's saving work. It is also perfectly clear that (canonized) holiness is intrinsically related to this total gift of self, because in fact it is only into these vessels, which stand completely free for him, that God can pour his charisms, only such men that he can shape into models (*canones*) of holiness before the eyes of the whole Church. But models exist in order to be applied: one who embodies *perfect* love, which does not seek that which is its own either spiritually or bodily, but is selfless and renunciatory, in the secular state of life, in marriage, and professional work, is certainly also "perfect" and "holy".

but an answer to Christ's deed of love and will therefore not be bound to any time; it will *always* be modern, since all ages are in equal need of this sign). Above all, he will not speculate (d) about whether the effects of this self-gift will be visible, for the fruit lies with God and cannot be calculated in a worldly sense; one can never say of the kingdom of God: "Lo, here it is!" or "There!" (Lk 17:21).

3. Nevertheless, this life of total self-gift is for all times the *great sign* in the Church and for the world, the sign that lets us see that God has given away everything for us in Christ, all the powers of spirit and body, and that it is possible to make such an answer in faith to this love that men, too, give away for God all that they have. But in order that this deed may not be an act that man takes upon himself (and also to avoid Pharisaism vis-à-vis those who do not perform it in the same way), it can be dared from the very beginning only as the response to a *call.* Thus it was for Abraham, Moses, Samuel, John the Baptist, the first disciples, Paul; thus it has been and will be throughout the millennia for those called ever afresh to a life of renunciation for their brethren, whether in the priestly or religious life or even in the midst of the world. A few comments ought to be made about this latter possibility.

4. *Secular Institutes*

The Church approved a modern form of the life of the counsels in 1947 and gave it its own status in canon law, namely, that of the "secular institutes". Their main idea is the union of secular (lay) state of life and professional work with the total gift of self or consecration (*consecratio*) that is characterized by the evangelical counsels. Already in the early period of the Church, consecrated virgins and men lived in the midst of the community and in their families. Great founders like Francis and Ignatius did not originally intend the foundation of "Orders" as such, but of groups of consecrated laymen in the midst of the world, who were not to be externally distinguished from their fellowmen and were to be for them a model and a provocation. In the Middle Ages, knightly Orders combined the life of the counsels with the life of war at the service of Christianity, colonization, hospitality, and the service of the sick. Great women at the beginning of the modern period—like Angela Merici and Mary Ward—had the breadth of vision to anticipate today's forms. When monastic life became impossible in the French Revolution, Father de Clorivière was the first ever to establish male and female communities, which we could consider the real beginnings of the secular institutes. These have multiplied especially since the beginning of the twentieth century, despite many opposing currents set in motion by the old Orders and the hesitation of the Curia. They showed themselves to be viable in the period between the Wars, and they were approved definitively after the Second World War. Numerous foundations on all continents[4] have still to survive trial by fire; many varieties exist—conservative and revolutionary—and per-

[4] Jean Beyer, *Les Instituts séculiers* (Paris: Desclée de Brouwer, 1954); H. A. Timmermann, *Die Weltgemeinschaften im deutschen Sprachraum*, Der neue Weg, vol. 2 (Einsiedeln: Johannes Verlag, 1963) with bibliography (out of print).

haps not all will prove to be viable. But the fundamental idea, approved by the Church, is already an inalienable part of her life.

It is in fact not at all obvious why a young man who wants to consecrate his whole existence to God and to the kingdom of God in the world must therefore leave the "world", enter a monastery, and study theology. He can do this, of course: the traditional forms of life of the Orders and congregations are not in the least dead; many of them are just as vigorous today as in the past; many of them carry out an activity that is indispensable for the Church. But they do not constitute the only possible form of the life of the counsels. Something analogous is true of the priesthood. Vocations to the service of the Church in the pastoral care of the faithful must be encouraged and cared for today more than ever; at most, one ought to make it clear to the candidates in the seminaries that their vocation, too, demands a total gift of their life to the service of the Church, that is, a form of life that cannot be essentially different from the life of the counsels. But not everyone who wishes to consecrate his life to the kingdom of God need become a parish priest in order to care for a community of believers. Perhaps he would prefer to collaborate in a professional milieu consisting mostly of unbelievers or at least people who have distanced themselves from the Church, thus penetrating into strata of the population that are virtually inaccessible to priests and religious. Why should he not live out the image of a man totally consecrated to God as a doctor, lawyer, journalist, politician, architect, engineer, technician, or member of any other secular profession, thus proving that he can be no less a worker, but also no less a fellow human being, who is altogether normal and not in any way eccentric?

All the *objections* to this form of life, at least when they come from Christians, are ill-considered and shortsighted. These objections are directed mainly against virginity and obedience; poverty offers fewer vulnerabilities to attack. Is the man who remains unmarried (for the sake of *God*, not out of egoism!) a psychological cripple—a charge that could be laid on all priests and religious, too—someone who lacks an essential sphere of experience? If that were the case, then Christ himself and his Mother would not be human beings of full value, and one would have to refuse to trust Paul's teaching about sexuality and marriage as well as most of the saints in the Church's history. This objection is understandable when it is made by non-Christians who have only psychology as a basis; but Christians ought to know that Christian love is not bodiless but unites the entire human being with the God who has become man ("the body is for the Lord . . . and the Lord for the body": 1 Cor 6:13), so that those who love with a truly Christian love possess an integral human experience thanks to the grace of Christ, something that can be seen quite unproblematically in every *good* confessor or spiritual father. The fact that a virginal life for the sake of God in the midst of the world will attract attention and cause surprise and offense belongs of course to the character of such an existence as an apostolic sign. In the case of priests and religious, we have (wrongly) grown so much accustomed to virginity that we scarcely notice it any more. But if a colleague in one's secular profession remains unmarried for the sake of Christ—how strange it is! It forces one to reflect: Is Christianity so much alive that it can still achieve such things today?

The objection to obedience is no less virulent. Can a man who is competent in a secular profession allow another man to prescribe something for him in the name of God? Answer: (1) One who has placed his *whole* existence (not just the "spiritual" half of it) at God's disposal and then chooses a course of study and a profession out of this attitude (in consultation with his superior) is one who carries out this professional work in obedience, together with all the responsibility it lays on his shoulders, and who places his secular activity, including that for which he himself must take responsibility, under the sacrifice and the grace of Christian obedience. (2) It goes without saying that the superior who has directed him to this professional work thereby himself assumes responsibility for doing so and cannot arbitrarily "shift around" the one who has received this commission (as one can order a missionary in an Order from place to place, for example). But the one who is obedient remains "available" for the whole of his life, and, through everything, his initial act of perfect readiness never dies.

We have already come to see that this "new" life is neither a "halfway" entity (compared to the integrity of the old Orders) nor something watered down; to the contrary, we ought to say that it is more difficult, because the man in question must continually unite two things in his existence: total dedication to God and total dedication to the world and his work. Naturally, each will nourish the other: his work makes his prayer come alive, and prayer deepens his involvement in the world. The equilibrium is never achieved once and for all; one must struggle ever anew to attain it. It is much more difficult here than perhaps in monasteries or rectories to "come to rest". Everything depends on whether the right spirit is unshakably alive; were it to die, then the institutional framework, too, would soon collapse. The new form of life is in a very direct way "leaven" in the great dough of the world; it embodies Church, not in a static way, but in a dynamic manner, extending frontiers, not through the organizations of "Catholic Action", but through the quiet involvement of individual personalities who preach more through their existence than through their word and who do so most profoundly, not through what they "portray" externally (as a sign of the kingdom of God), but through what they accomplish internally, in secret, through their quiet sacrifice.

The time may very well come—it is probably much closer than most of us think—when unbelief could take over the reins of government even in our West, even in our own country, so that there would be no monasteries and perhaps not even any longer a normally functioning clergy. Then, even more than today, would the hour of the secular institutes come. But this hour has already come today, in a manner audible to all those who have not let their ear be lulled by the "old song" of fond tradition. It is no longer possible to think of ecclesial life in Italy, Spain, France, or America without the secular institutes; for these are surely the countries in which we find more courage, Christian imagination, and spiritual élan in the young people than among us. But it is of course true that this new form of life ought not to be defended, or taken on, primarily out of considerations of "what it brings", external expediency, or Church politics. This happens in some places, casting an unfavorable light on the whole business. Even this new reality must have its roots as deep as possible in revelation—all the way into the heart of the New Testament (which recapitulates the Old): all the way into the heart of God's crucified love, which demands a response.

IV.

LAY MOVEMENTS IN THE CHURCH

1. The Situation of the Catholic Lay Movements Today

a. On the origins of lay movements in the Church

The words that provide the foundation for understanding lay movements in the Church are found in the First Letter to the Corinthians: "Now there are varieties of gifts, but the same Spirit. . . . To each is given the manifestation of the Spirit for the common good [of the whole Church]. . . . All these are inspired by one and the same Spirit, who apportions to each one individually as he wills" (12:4, 7, 11). Even a summary review of the Church's history will confirm this characteristic, which is astonishing because it points us back to the transcendental, incalculable origin of the Spirit's charisms, an origin that cannot be domesticated. The three aspects that this passage both distinguishes and holds together—(1) the variety of spiritual gifts; (2) the fact that they are ordered to the benefit of the entire Church; and (3) their spontaneous birth from the divine Spirit, not from some human calculation—are already clearly to be seen in the first few centuries of the Church: it is not in the least a flight from the world that sends the layman Anthony of

Egypt into the wilderness; rather it is his desire to help the Church through prayer and asceticism; he frequently returns to the city, and a great movement of disciples is spontaneously brought to life by his existence. The same is true of the great charisms of the layman Benedict, later of the layman Francis of Assisi, and later still that of the layman Ignatius Loyola: no one other than the Holy Spirit urges them to set out on their journey and leads them to their goal, often by lengthy, circuitous routes upon which they must allow themselves to be blindly led. If the great movements they kindled into life became partly or wholly clerical communities later on, for both internal and external reasons, nevertheless their lay and purely pneumatic origin ought never to be forgotten.

We can also see this pneumatic origin in the fact that the second element mentioned above, the visible incorporation into the universal Church—in practice, papal approbation—sometimes took a very long time, until sufficient proof had been given of the movement's genuine supernatural provenance and thereby also of its Catholic orientation. There could also be problematic, indeed, tragic cases, such as some of the movements for poverty started by laymen in the Middle Ages, whose charismatic origin drove them out of the visible Church, sometimes through the impatience of the members and sometimes also through a lack of insight on the part of the hierarchy, so that they were not able to bear all the fruit that was intended. The Poverello possessed both the necessary patience and the almost boundless reverence for ecclesiastical authority that were needed to ensure for his movement its proper place in the Church's structure and, indeed, to fortify this place through his own, deeply personal sacrifices.

We must not let ourselves be confused by two things in this initial overview: first, by the distinction (justified in canon law and in theology) between "Orders" (and congregations, and so forth), on the one hand, and lay movements, on the other; a perfectly legitimate development from the one to the other may have taken place, as for example in the Society of Jesus. But second, one ought not at all to encourage the view that all the charismatic movements in the Church are originally inspired by the Spirit in a layman; such movements can be founded in an equally original manner by priests or bishops, as for example the community of Saint Basil or Saint Bruno or Saint Norbert, or by canons regular (Dominic) or members of an Order (Bernard). The Holy Spirit is free to distribute his gifts to whomever and through whomever he wills.

But what we can already learn from this observation is that original charisms genuinely—and, from this perspective, always incalculably and surprisingly—stem from the Spirit; they cannot be called into being by the Church merely because she thinks they would be useful(!). This does not prevent a bishop from gathering a group of suitable and willing laymen to help him in his diocesan concerns and entrusting them with particular tasks, and still less does it prevent a pope from planning movements of laymen on a larger scale, conceiving of these movements and organizing them from the very outset within a hierarchical framework, perhaps preferring to classify them according to a rational plan in sociological groups: young men and girls, men and women, or workers and intellectuals, and so forth. Both bishop and pope can be led in such endeavors by an inspiration of the Holy Spirit. Nevertheless, looking back over history, one can surely say that the foundations that were brought about by the hierarchy on the basis of rational considerations may have answered a need of the moment but do not display the same penetrating force as the spontaneous movements we mentioned above, which the Holy Spirit calls forth.

We mention only in passing the possibility, which has existed historically and still remains, for laymen to find their place within the sphere lit up by the great charism out of which an Order has developed (in so-called Third Orders). Indeed, they have often had all the more right to do so since, as we have seen, the original charism of the founder did not point to the foundation of an Order as such but to the renewal of the Church's spirit in general.

But it was necessary to wait until our own century to see such a blossoming and variety of autonomous lay movements in the Church, some of which may indeed take their orientation from great charisms of the past but most of which have emerged from new, independent inspirations of the Holy Spirit. The spontaneous development of this rich abundance confronts the Church with some new problems: How is she to preserve and promote the individual movements in the true Catholic spirit; how is she to maintain, without external pressure and the imposition of institutionalization, the connection of each movement with the Church as a whole and also with other movements, those of a similar and those of a different kind; how can she preserve within her own unity this spontaneously irrupting multiplicity, mindful of what the Gospel says about the miraculous catch of fish: "Peter hauled the net ashore, full of large fish . . . and although there were so many, the net was not torn" (Jn 21:11)?

b. Lay movements and the ecclesial "states of life"

It seems worthwhile to say something here at the beginning about the question of their relationship to the ecclesial "states of life". Although we put quotation marks around this word, which today is often referred to as medieval and obsolete, it retains its relevance despite all its limitations, or more precisely, despite its imprecision. The specification of the official priesthood, which one acquires through the conferral of the sacrament of priestly ordination, remains precise, but the relationship between the lay "state" and the "state" of the counsels has become fluid; the clearest expression of the latter is religious life, and its form of life includes in various nuances the congregations and other forms (often institutionalized only in part) in which the evangelical counsels are lived out. Persons in these forms of life are not customarily called laymen. But every layman in the Church is free to bind himself to the evangelical counsels for a period, or for the whole of his life, through private vows; this is done by the officially recognized secular institutes and also (in the form of a contract) by the members of the Personal Prelature of Opus Dei, and all of these attach great value (which the Church recognizes) to their status as laymen.

It is therefore not surprising that today there exist many

members in a number of lay movements who dedicate themselves within the movement to a life according to the evangelical counsels; it is also not surprising that the greater amount of time they can make available for the concerns of the movement makes them a kind of backbone. Whether or not they consider themselves members of a "secular institute" (in the institutional sense) ought not to matter to the movement, since they remain laymen among laymen.

Another question arises when an open lay movement wishes to receive priests and religious as members or sympathizers. Priests can be true members of a movement only with the approval of their bishop; they can also be appointed by the hierarchy as spiritual assistants or counselors for the movement, and regulations have been laid down for this case.[1] In the same way, religious will be able to take part in a movement with the knowledge of their superiors, who must always reflect on the extent to which such a membership either gives new life to their own religious charism or else might perhaps make their relationship to this charism unclear.

One must avoid all formalism in the mutual relationship of the "states of life"—for it is precisely in their differences that they exist totally for each other and are therefore open to each other—and, by the same token, one must pay heed to the specificity of the charism

[1] Pontifical Council for the Laity, *Priests in Associations of the Laity* (Vatican City, 1981). This text emphasizes forcefully the fact that the priest must fulfill his priestly functions without compromise in such movements: this is what the laity expect of him, and only so does he act in keeping with his vocation.

bestowed on the individual and designated for him, so that superficial intermixtures may be avoided.

c. Reasons for the development of lay movements today

It is impossible to foresee how the radical new movements that the Holy Spirit brings about in a particular age will take place; yet one may hope for them and expect them, in view of the spiritual distress of an age and of the Church in this age. Thus the charisms that are blossoming today in the sphere of the lay movements and in other areas of the Church are just as unforeseeable as at earlier periods, but one can certainly indicate the reasons they may be taking place precisely today.

Although many of them had their start before the Second Vatican Council, the Council's image of the Church no doubt gave a powerful reinforcement to their development. The idea—which of course was only ever an impression—that Christian perfection was reserved to the religious state and that the layman in the world must be content with a secondary form of Christian existence has collapsed thanks to the powerful declaration, faithful to the Gospels, that all Christians are equally called to holiness, those who live and are active in the world no less than religious and priests, the married no less than the unmarried. This programmatic principle is surely the reason why Christians who aim for perfection have no longer joined a Third Order in such great numbers as before but instead have formed themselves into independent structures within the Church, even when drawing on the spirituality of one particular Order. It is in fact possible in some places to see the opposite of what happened previously, namely that the new lay movements exert a decisive influence on religious communities and are able to rejuvenate their spirit.

A second point can be mentioned here, which is connected with the tendencies of the last Council, that is, its *aggiornamento* in the best and most ecclesial sense of the word: the rediscovery and rethinking of the Church's original mission to the secular world, especially since its secularization and technological developments have made the world something new that is doubly problematic for the Church. In the course of the Church's turn to her total mission, it goes without saying that the Council would turn especially to the laity and call to mind their mediating position between the world and Church, a position more indispensable than ever. Considered from within the Church, the form-giving hierarchy and the edifying service of office may be as essential as ever, and the Church's secret hope for the effectiveness of her apostolate may rest as much as ever on the prayer, the penance, and the active involvement of the Orders; but for the acknowledged necessity of mediating to the world and for the inculturation of Christianity into the structures and ways of thinking of the world, it cannot be denied that the program of the Dogmatic Constitution on the Church (*Lumen Gentium*) and the Pastoral Constitution on the Church in the Modern World (*Gaudium et Spes*) shifted the laity into a kind of central position. The laity had always had its home in this "in-between", so that the Council did not occasion any crisis of self-understanding for them as it did for certain Orders, which were indeed already apostolic but thought that they had to acquire a new profile for themselves by coming closer to the world and becoming secularized in certain ways, and as it did for many priests, too, who, finding vocation to be somewhat out of touch with real life, thought they had to make efforts—often exaggerated and unnatural—to become "adapted to the world". The powerful ecclesial crisis that followed the Council, which was, on the one hand, a crisis of secularization and, on the other hand, a crisis of the understanding of authority in the Church, affected the priestly and the religious states even in the theology both produced to an incomparably greater extent than it did the lay state, which had no reason to reflect on its identity or to "call it into question". This difference has been reflected in a very clear and practical way in the way these respective states have related to the Church in the last few years: the overwhelming majority of conflicts have been initiated by clergy and religious and can sometimes involve certain groups of laity in their cause, whereas the lay movements we have been discussing—it must be admitted—have remained altogether immune to these attacks of fever. They are ecclesial in a straightforward manner, accepting the hierarchical leadership of the Church without protest, but they are not slaves, for the simple reason that the directives issued by the hierarchy are less and less willing to intrude in questions that fall under the laity's competence: the revision of Galileo's trial was intended to portray this symbolically.

A third reason can be discerned for the timeliness of the lay movements that have sprung from their own charisms. In a transitional period, the hierarchy had the breadth of vision to recognize the necessity of allowing the laity to carry out their mediatory function but bound this function tightly to the hierarchy as though it alone—and not the Church as a whole—were responsible for the mission to the world. The result was that the lay associations that the Church eagerly set in motion were at first able to bring about a very considerable influence, but this, however, noticeably decreased with the years, so that the structures that were originally set up could be kept alive only artificially, through the Church's external "fuel supply". Since in some countries new movements enjoy the benevolent support of bishops who take an interest in them, while in others the bishops hold fast to the earlier organizations, founded and supported more directly by the hierarchy, conflicts may arise here that can be resolved only through an attitude of patience within the ranks of the hierarchy and through a totally ecclesial attitude on the part of the new movements, as well as through a spirit of reconciliation and perhaps even cooperation among the members of the movements. Genuine competition in religious commitment will not damage either form of movement, but anything that could divide dioceses and parishes must be avoided.

d. The specific mission of the laity as mediators between Church and world

After what has been said, the role of the layman in the Church appears in a new light. Since professional competence is more important than ever in the countless, immensely complex questions that face humanity on a world scale—questions not merely of development, but of bare survival in the immediate future—the laity, who combine such a competence with a genuine Christian sensibility, move into the front line of the Church's missionary task as well. Previously it was clergy who stood in this front line, as committed proclaimers of the faith, and their role here is still undisputed in many countries with a rather simpler culture. But the influences of the technological and economic global civilization are infiltrating those countries too, bringing with them problems that once again call for the specialist, the layman.

The norms and solutions offered by faith and by theology for humanity's questions are certainly fundamental and are as obligatory for the Christian layman as they are for non-Christians outside the Church. But it would be presumptuous for the priest and the theologian to want to direct the translation of faith-driven principles into the economic, political, and cultural spheres themselves. To take just one example from many: only laymen with a thorough professional training, not in the least theologians, are competent to articulate what is urgently required to deal in an adequate way with the Latin American questions of economics and urbanization. This example is not meant to conceal the many other fields of work where well-trained Christian laymen are often desperately needed; once again, we mention only a few other examples: such as the professional field of journalism, of the mass media, of ecology, politics, and so forth. It is here that the important decisions for mankind's survival and well-being are to be made.

Two things should not be overlooked here: first, the

silent and unnoticed involvement of countless laymen who do not occupy positions where such decisions affecting the culture of the whole world are being made; they form the indispensable background that makes it possible for gifted and responsible individuals to emerge. They can only come from families in which they have been educated to take such a responsible attitude by mothers and fathers, brothers and sisters and teachers. Every level of society and all the professions must be permeated by the yeast of courageous Christians who are sure of their faith.

These in turn—this is the second point—demand the effective presence of educated priests, diocesan or religious, who live out the faith convincingly and preach it, as well as the prayer and renunciation of many contemplatives who live in relative or total hiddenness. The message of Lisieux, which is so clear in this regard, has lost nothing of its relevance. Self-sacrificing prayer is the inner motor that drives all of the activity in the outer and outermost ranks, which have to struggle for the faith and its effectiveness in truly secularized spheres.

To be sure, there are certain personalities capable of uniting the priesthood to a secular profession. But to speak more generally, this union will no doubt be meaningful only where a specifically or prevalently sacerdotal task is brought into the field of a secular interest, as for example with the worker-priests of the past and the present, or in professional fields where it could become significant, for example, in the potential and desirable union of psychotherapy and pastoral care (with the power of absolution). As a whole, this will remain the exception, whereas the normal model will still be that of the layman counseled in religious questions by an experienced pastor.

This perspective, imposed by the present state of the world, suggests in its turn associations of Christian laymen, associations that are defined and structured by the laity's ever more clearly emerging task of mediation. This does not mean that former kinds of associations for purely religious purposes, such as the "Marian congregations" in the period from the seventeenth to the nineteenth century, have become meaningless—certainly not; but they must be complemented by new lay movements, which can bear the religious impulses more purposefully out into their respective fields of work. This can take place in very different ways according to the field of work and also to the individual charisms, as the great variety of such movements shows; absolutely uniform directives for all are therefore impossible. But it ought to be possible to draw up certain guidelines that the individual movements should at least take into consideration, so that they may be put into practice in an analogous manner, in keeping with the specific character of each movement. We shall attempt to do this in what follows.

2. *Aspects of the Spirituality of Lay Movements*

a. *Many missions within the one faith*

The biblical directive we took as our starting point not only tolerates but positively demands the multiplicity of "members" and missions within the unity of faith that belongs to the one mystical "Body" of Christ. The multiplicity already in the concrete expressions of faith is itself possible because faith can contemplate the depth and fullness of God's self-revealing truth in which it believes from ever new sides but can never exhaust it. Despite the inscrutability of God's decisions and the inconceivability of his ways (cf. Rom 11:33), the contours of revelation are anything but vague and arbitrary; they possess clearly defined and unchangeable features, as the central figure of Jesus Christ shows. The fundamental lines can be clearly discerned: from Christ the incarnate, crucified, and risen one, we have the image of the triune God, the figure of the Church that comes forth from him and bears witness to him, with her faith, her ministry, her sacraments, her relationship to the Old Covenant and to world history in general and to Mary as the chosen representative of Israel and of humanity in her consent to the Incarnation of the Son of God, and finally the insight that the world is created by a good God, the insight into his providence and into the fulfillment that creation hopes for in him. One must always keep this totality (here sketched only by way of allusions) in view. No charism would deserve our credence if it made a single aspect (for example, the Marian or the eucharistic aspect) so central in its spirituality that it pushed aside the fundamental supporting pillars of the faith and these lost their claim on the believer's full attention.

The situation of lay movements in their relationship to the faith, which nourishes their piety, is not easy. Contemporary theology raises hundreds of questions that, at least when looked at from the outside, appear to put a question mark (at least methodologically) to all that has been valid hitherto. It is not possible for the layman to investigate to what extent these questions are warranted in every single case; and thus he is inclined to take a fundamentalist position that accords the same weight to every statement directly or indirectly concerning the faith, a position that lacks the legitimate nuances of perspective that have been elaborated by theological research. Sometimes, though less often, he is also open to the arguments of a theology that is "liberal" in the problematic sense, especially in ecumenical dialogues wherein he would like to meet his partner halfway. This is why it is crucial for Catholic lay movements to assure themselves of a good theologian who is also well acquainted with modern questions posed in theology and exegesis, so that he can instruct the members on essential questions, counsel them on individual topics, and test and enliven their faith from time to time in courses and days of recollection.

So much for the objective contents of the faith (*fides quæ creditur*). As for the subjective act of faith (*fides qua creditur*), in face of the increasing dechristianization of their social milieu, many laymen will probably run the risk of being shaken in faith by chasing after a psychological "experience" of what they believe, either together in group-dynamic exercises or singly in contemplation or meditation techniques that are not seldom influenced by Eastern methods of contemplation. Here, too, it is easy to see why the layman who hungers for a particular experience needs prudent counseling by experienced pastors. We Christians believe primarily because of the proclamation of the gospel; its mysteries may and indeed should appear highly plausible to us, but no subjective experience can supersede its mystery character and open it up completely. The greatest caution must be used when applying the concept of experience to the faith; it is most convincingly used when a Christian confirms the rightness of his turn to the gospel over time. But we should be no less critical of attempts to effect a synthesis between Christian adoration and thanksgiving and Eastern meditative techniques: as the Church Fathers already knew, some things can be helpful for inner recollection, but other things would surely undermine the sheer encounter with the loving God. As Holy Scripture shows, Christian prayer is always addressed to the living God. It is never the search for one's own "self" or for the transcendental ego.

b. Challenges facing lay movements' spiritualities

It follows immediately from what has been said above that every participant in a Catholic lay movement needs a theological education suited to his state of life. This will scarcely be possible without the guidance of a person of proven worth.

A sufficient familiarity with Sacred Scripture is fundamental; the Bible circles that are so popular today can be a good first step, but they are very much in need of guidance if they are not to get sidetracked, even—and precisely—where group discussions about a text and the impression it makes on each individual are central. The Bible is an unimaginably many-faceted totality, and its individual statements must always be read and interpreted in the light of this totality; the as yet inexperienced layman has the tendency to cling to an individual statement, isolating and absolutizing something that takes on its true value only in relationship to other texts. Even a whole group of similarly inexperienced people will not find the right access to this: someone who is more competent must recall the larger contexts for them.

Something similar is true of personal dealings with the Bible in reading, prayer, and study, but here a good commentary can assume the work of guidance; there are enough of these today. The edition of the Jerusalem Bible with footnotes should be mentioned because of the simplicity and clarity of its apparatus.

A deeper familiarity with the Bible will help guard against the danger we mentioned above of absolutizing the special charism of the movement in such a way that one is no longer sufficiently aware that it is essentially a member of a greater whole, of the *Catholica*.

The layman requires such guidance in his dealings with the Bible so that he may have enough distance and confidence vis-à-vis the countless questions raised by historical-critical exegesis. He ought to be brought to a point where he is no longer afraid of these questions and learns to distinguish between, first of all, the numerous positive fruits of research, which has also provided many insights that are fruitful for spirituality, and, secondly, the innumerable hypotheses that are consciously proposed as such by scholarship and ought not to be accepted immediately by non-specialists as firm results, and, thirdly, unacceptable assertions that are often presented with a force suggesting they are proven facts but that undermine the central mysteries of the faith. By no means should the layman get the impression, from a superficial knowledge of exegesis, that everything today has grown unsteady. This is simply untrue; but in order to grasp this point, one needs some knowledge of the distinctions mentioned above. An experienced specialist can help a person to acquire such knowledge.

And only then is it possible to combine a necessary knowledge with a prayerful contemplation of the biblical text without any difficulties. Such a contemplative reading is, moreover, indispensable for the layman, if his praying is not to remain stuck at the subjective, indeed, often at the infantile level. Childlikeness in the gospel sense —a fundamental quality of good prayer—has nothing in common with this immaturity, which distorts the father-child relationship by reducing it to egoistic opinions and wishes, whereas the true child of God always keeps in view the entire greatness of the love that has been revealed and demonstrated by the triune God.

Childlikeness in prayer can best be preserved when accompanied by adulthood and maturity in the judgment one makes about the multiplicity of the present-day currents in the Church. This judgment will not simply echo the slogan of pluralism (which may also embrace theology), which in fact means two things: that one ought to allow contradictory and incompatible opinions to hold sway in the Church without any criticism and, secondly, that the pronouncements of the authentic Magisterium may be regarded as one opinion among others. The first position destroys the particularity and the universal comprehensiveness of God's revelation in Jesus Christ, while the second destroys the function (derived from Christ and the apostles) of a particular official ministry guided by the Holy Spirit in the interpretation of this revelation. The truly mature layman will know how to distinguish between a legitimate variety of viewpoints within the one all-embracing catholicity of doctrine and the false interpretation of this variety as arbitrariness, that is, between genuine plurality and false pluralism.

Every Christian spirituality has its center in Jesus Christ as the incarnate revelation of the divine Father in the Holy Spirit: it knows of no "Jesus-worship" without the mystery of the Trinity. This is also true for any spirituality, such as the various shades of liberation theology, that wishes above all to seek practical expression in activity that aims at political, social, and economic liberation. Spiritualities with a Marian hue must not neglect to look on the person of Mary within the framework of which she is a part. A Church-centered spirituality cannot exist, for the Church is "only" the Body of Christ, and this Body would remain incomprehensible without a constant contemplation of the Head. The diverse functions within the Church to which many lay movements dedicate themselves can never as such stand in the center of a spirituality, since they are all nothing more than offshoots, initiated by the Holy Spirit, from the one center Jesus Christ, who remains the highest and completely normative revelation of the triune God in the world.

To impress this upon every member of a lay movement today in such a way that it becomes second nature is a task that belongs to the spirituality of every movement, the spirituality that must remain the constantly beating heart that gives life to all their actions.

c. The movement and the individual

The more the individual man feels threatened or even lost in modern mass civilization, the easier it is to understand his wanting to seek shelter in a community of like-minded people. This is not dangerous so long as the community helps its member to find his identity, thanks to which he can then hold his own as a single, indeed, as a solitary individual in an entirely alien milieu. Mutual strengthening in the consciousness of having a personal task, dialogue with like-minded people about difficulties and challenges, occasional collaboration of several persons who belong to the same movement: all this is perfectly correct and corresponds to the best spirit of a movement. The situation becomes dangerous only when the individual would find his identity and come to see his true self only within this particular experience of fellowship, which then seems to him to make concrete the true, living Church. This can at most be tolerated in an initial stage of belonging to the community, especially in the case of young people, but the leadership of the community must seek from the outset to develop the personality of the members in such a way that they can fulfill their task in the world autonomously and, perhaps, even in isolation.

It cannot be denied that the experience of being together collectively often awakens certain emotions that those present easily equate with genuine religious and ecclesial experience, so that subsequently, when they are alone, they cannot find their way either in prayer or in daily life. Being together may and should kindle joy and strengthen faith, but it ought not to present itself as an exclusive or even only a central model of Christian existence. Here, too, there lurks the danger mentioned above, of giving a psychological or sociological experience a religious and Christian interpretation without further qualification.

In some movements, this recurrent danger has led to a consequence that we must discuss separately, namely, that the movement, or the group that represents it in a particular locale, tends to look on itself as the genuine (precisely because "experienced") core of the local Church or parish and therefore, almost unconsciously, to separate itself from the rest of the faithful. Where the movement as such is aware of its responsibility for educating the individual's character and acts accordingly, there is much less danger of forming this kind of sect.

d. *The movement and the Church*

It has already been noted that the relationship of most of today's lay movements to the visible Church led by her official ministry is healthy and free of problems in comparison to other communities or groups of theologians. The highest representative of the Church has expressed his joy at this and has in turn placed his full confidence in the recognized movements. This fundamental openness to the whole Church, without distrust and the inappropriate search for things to criticize, is one of the most positive characteristics of the lay movements.

In order for this fruitful element to be able to survive and demonstrate its fruitfulness, several concrete perspectives must be kept in view.

The first can be formulated thus: The ecclesial office in its essential dimensions—its teaching, priestly, and governing office—is founded and accompanied by the Holy Spirit just as much as the more personal manifestations of the same Spirit. The objective holiness of the ecclesial structures is the abiding foundation that makes it possible for subjective holiness to unfold within them. This ought especially to be kept in mind by those movements that call themselves charismatic with a special emphasis. It is not possible for another charismatic hierarchy to exist alongside the official one (as in some movements outside the Church); nor is it possible to add other sacraments to those definitively defined by the Church; nor is it possible to make the efficacy of these sacraments dependent on conditions that are not universally recognized by the Church's theology. This is why these movements, which are important for the equilibrium of spirituality and which emphasize the ever present significance of the Holy Spirit, must remain especially transparent to the official Church—not merely to individual priests and bishops who make known their membership in the movement or their particular sympathy with it, but to a *Catholica* that some individuals may perhaps find not so Spirit-inspired as they would like. This openness is one of the criteria of the genuineness of all ecclesial charisms, as the example of the great saints irrefutably shows. What applies to the charismatic movements is the same that applies to every Catholic spirituality: namely, that the relationship to Christ must stand in the midpoint, for it is through him that we have access to the Father; we have received the Spirit through him and the Father; and it is the Spirit's mission to introduce us into the inexhaustible riches of Christ and to interpret him in the depth of his being and his word. The Spirit casts all his light on Christ: he does not draw separate and competing attention to himself. He can be praised, adored, implored, and in a certain sense experienced, but this alters nothing of his fundamental function and intention, "not to speak on his own authority" (Jn 16:13), but to speak from the one Word in God, which proceeds from the Father and has become man in Jesus Christ. He can generate enthusiasm in the hearers of the Word and exultation over its depths, but in doing so he does not call attention to himself.

A second aspect that must be kept in mind could follow precisely from the unquestioningly ecclesial attitude of the movements. It is possible that this attitude could lead a person to believe his own movement to be the pinnacle in living as Church and as Catholic and thus to recommend it to others with a missionary zeal. Some movements have a triumphalistic tone of which they themselves are unconscious. To caricature it somewhat crudely: "Come to us and you will find the fullness of Catholicism in its most relevant form." It is normal that movements would look out for new members and that they would try to make their spiritual riches visible when they recruit. But there can be forms here that transgress the limits of discretion, even if only slightly. We are speaking here only of lay movements and exclude the question of how the Orders and congregations and secular institutes recruit their members. Since lay movements are open sociological groups that everyone can recognize, they are also accessible to anyone who is suited to their goals and is prepared to commit himself to them. In themselves, the movements are not esoteric or exclusive, although considered from the outside, they are often too quick to stamp themselves with an isolationist label, so that mere observers look on them with a critical eye. Transparency about their ecclesial and cultural program and the way it is lived out in the lives of their members is essential if they are to have success, indeed, if they are to have a rightful place in the Church.

A problem emerges in this context only when—as often happens—a number of members at the center bind themselves more closely to the path of discipleship indicated by Christ, in the form of a definitive decision to follow the evangelical counsels. Whether or not they are recognized by canon law, such core groups then form something like a secular institute and need a specific institutionalized framework that does apply in this specificity to the rest of the members; if it seems right to them, they can appeal to the discretion that is customary in the institutes with regard to their (private) commitment. (As we have said, every layman is entitled to bind himself privately in this way, but if others happen to discover that he has done so, ecclesial love will not shine a spotlight on him and thus discredit him in the eyes of those who do not understand or who do not share the faith.) The boundaries between secular institutes, which were founded as such and perhaps have a looser circle of laymen around themselves, and lay movements, whose own development leads to the formation of a core group analogous to the institutes, are certainly fluid today. Both developments are possible, and in both it will be necessary to pose the question of transparency to the entire Church, indeed to the public sphere, and to work out an appropriate solution.

New questions arise when we consider the existence of a group of people belonging to a movement in relation to a particular parish and diocese. To begin with, the movement will be put to the severe test of whether it acknowledges the catholicity of the larger community and makes itself available to promote the life of this community—or whether it is so convinced of its own catholicity that it adopts a polemical attitude toward other movements that perhaps work in the same parish or diocese. The existence of movements with and alongside one another in one limited area of the Church places high Christian demands on the various groups: first, they must accept the validity of other programs, priorities, and charisms, to the extent that the Christian discernment of spirits makes this at all possible; then, in circumstances where this is possible and feasible, a mutual promotion for the greater good of the larger whole (the small parish or the large diocese) of which both are a part. Corresponding demands are made of the parish priest and the bishop: they must remain objective as they test the values that belong to the different movements, not allowing themselves to be biased by personal preferences and prejudices and being concerned as much as possible to enable the peaceful collaboration of the movements. It ought not to happen that one larger and recognized movement is shown so much favor by parish priests and bishops of particular dioceses that there is no space for other movements to grow or that they find so much opposition they cannot engage in their activity. But in their impartiality, the bishop and the parish priest are also obliged to carry out discernment of spirits, and it could be their duty at some point to call to order movements that act all too triumphalistically, as if they were the sole means of salvation.

e. The movement and the world

Much of what has been said above applies to this new theme as well, above all the demand that the intentions and plans of a movement be transparent also to those who believe differently or who do not believe at all. This transparency has of course boundaries, both above and below. It need not cast discretion aside and divulge its inner spirit and all its structures and forms before the eyes of the whole world—but still less ought it to appear as a kind of secret society or a Catholic Freemasonry with a variety of initiatory stages, for it will usually be presumed that all this merely camouflages a lust for power, and the movement will inevitably call forth many hostilities. In reality, a healthy middle path is certainly possible here, a path that must be followed in spite of being obstructed by the misunderstandings and false interpretations that can be expected again and again. It has become so normal for most people today to be involved in some social or political work that a committed involvement in a lay movement with a specific goal (but one that is comprehensible, if not acceptable, to everyone) does not stamp its members as sectarian.

It is of the essence of lay movements that they bring the spirit of the Church into the affairs of the world, and this is why part of their program will increasingly consist in the translation of this ecclesial spirit into a healthy culture of their own people and of all humanity. The inner religious life of their members will be less their exclusive concern than it was in the confraternities or Marian congregations; rather, they will focus on both the religious education and cultural activity of their members. The movements will not interfere in the professional area of the individual member but will be concerned to see that he remains open as much to the world as to Christian concerns. A capacity for dialogue ought to be a concern for all the leaders of such movements, whether this means ecumenical dialogue with non-Catholic Christians or dialogue with those of other faiths. Such dialogues, often difficult, are part of the daily bread of Christian laymen today in their places of work and elsewhere. This bread must be broken in a human way together with their fellows. One will not learn this art of dialogue without some training; if such training is lacking, the lay movement will end up contradicting its proper essence by closing in upon itself. This is why each one ought to acquire an appropriate knowledge of other world views and learn to discern which points in them are compatible with one's own world view, where the differences lie, and what can lead to damaging developments for human culture. It may be that conversations among members, where some are more versed in the culture of dialogue than others, can accomplish more here than all-too-theoretical courses.

It is up to the imagination of each movement to decide which forms of cultural activity seem most fruitful for a particular country or cultural milieu: political or journalistic activity, involvement in publishing, scientific work in research or teaching, economics, and so forth. Naturally, yet another delicate problem emerges when culturally rewarding posts are to be filled, and there is no simple formula to resolve this problem in every case: Ought the Christian (even as a layman) to strive with all his might for the "first place" and seek to conquer the most efficient positions of power? Ought he, at least in some respect, to make use of all means ethically justifiable, so that when it is a question of filling a particularly important post, for example, he should award this to a member of the movement rather than to another suitable candidate? Whatever may be said in each individual case, a Christian movement ought not to get anywhere near the odor of the lust for power. It should always keep in mind that the proper staffing of middle and subordinate posts (the "ground-level") is just as decisive for a culture as having the leading posts.

All that has been said here, of course, holds good only for countries in which lay movements can develop unhindered. In countries in which this is not the case, where such movements are either totally prohibited or limited specifically in their influence on the world, the inevitable conclusions will have to be drawn: this may entail the necessity of keeping the membership small or secret, of shifting the primary focus to personal religious education, or of deepening the art of the discernment of spirits.

f. Reciprocal relationships among movements

We have already touched repeatedly on the question of the reciprocal relationship of the numerous lay movements, each with its own specific characteristics. In the spirit of the *Catholica*, their physical coexistence must necessarily also be a spiritual coexistence. Given the narrowness of human consciousness, this will not always be easy. It will demand of each movement a renunciation of claims to absoluteness and often a serious strength of mind.

But already the first common meetings in recent years have brought surprisingly positive results, making possible a spontaneous mutual encounter and mutual understanding in the common sphere of the Church. When each movement presents itself, and in the subsequent shared conversation, each movement discovers in the others values that it lacks or that are underdeveloped; one receives a very concrete lesson in what Paul means with his metaphor of the body and the limbs that complement each other; one recognizes one's own limitations and the necessity and usefulness of what the others are doing. And since one cannot do everything oneself, and cannot assimilate all that belongs to others, one learns to acknowledge the others without jealousy. In particular, those groups ordered to activity in the world come to understand how indispensable contemplation is, and those who are concerned too much with their own interior life or some special devotion are exhorted to open themselves further, in keeping with the layman's vocation. The echo of these first international meetings is so great that it calls for increased contact on the national and regional levels, too.

It ought also to be possible to learn from Church history. The foundations of new Orders seldom took place without resistance, suspicions, and delays; some time was needed, not only before they were universally recognized, but also for mutual contact to become more natural in a Christian sense and in a Christian spirit. On the other hand, throughout the centuries there have always been foundations that proved to be fruitful only for a period and then disappeared again. Not everything that is blossoming today need remain valid for centuries; there exist fainter charisms, more superficial groups, which answer a transient purpose, quickly shoot up, and then die. Others may have to struggle perhaps for decades with difficulties that may be imposed on them by God as their starting capital. This is why one should not be hasty in passing judgment on others in mutual encounters; large numbers are not a sufficient argument for depth and penetrative force; many things must absolutely remain small in numbers in order to have an effect—and the external success will be reserved for those who come later.

But the basic will for collaboration is surely an infallible sign of the genuinely Catholic spirit. One may justly raise a question about the spirituality of one who, as a matter of principle, stays away from every meeting and common work.

One final point: the movements have different structures. No movement can exist without a minimum of structure; one needs a formulated goal, precisely defined expectations of the members, meetings that are announced in advance, and so forth. Now, there are a number of strong movements that have gathered entirely around the personality of the founder and have organized themselves according to his directives. These can attain a marvelous flourishing, but if their internal structuring remains at the minimum described above, they run the risk of falling apart when the leading personality dies. It may be that providence intends precisely this; but it may also be the case that providence desires the movement to persevere, and this can be made possible if some institutional structures are set up in time. These structures would include not only organizational regulations, but certainly also directives that tap into the spiritual depths and look beyond what is relevant specifically to the present day. Sometimes the excessively central role of one particular personality, who has been able to fascinate a great number of young people, has hindered the continued existence of a genuine charism.

But open movements cannot be forced into a closed system of ideas. They can be fully justified in the diversity of their provenance. Some are formed simply because a need for social involvement becomes visible somewhere in the world. There is no point in looking for a properly supernatural charism here, since the common activity of Christians corresponds straightforwardly to their sense of responsibility in a specific situation. Others come into being through the charism of a founder; still others—like the charismatic movements—through a general impulse of the Spirit, which need not be bound to one particular personality. But the variety of these origins is no argument against a closer or looser collaboration within the sphere of the *Catholica* and in her spirit.

FIRST PUBLICATION REFERENCES

The articles in this book were first published in other publications, as follows:

A Life Held in Readiness for God: "Une vie livrée à Dieu", in *Vie consacrée* 43, no. 1 (Brussels, 1971), 5–23. = "Gottbereites Leben. Über den Sinn des Rätelebens heute", in *Bulletin Unione Internazionale Superiori Generali* 1, no. 21 (Rome: UISG, 1971), 11–21.

The Layman in the Life of the Counsels: *Der Laie und der Ordensstand. Christ heute* Series 1/2 (Einsiedeln: Johannes Verlag, 1948; 2d ed., Freiburg: Herder, 1949; 9th ed. 1989).

The Essence and Significance of Secular Institutes: "Wesen und Tragweite der Säkularinstitute", in *Civitas: Monatsschrift des Schweiz. Studentenvereins*, 11 (1956), Special Number, *Der Laie in der Kirche*, 196–210.

On the Theology of the State of the Counsels: "Zur Theologie des Rätestandes", in Stephan Richter, ed., *Das Wagnis der Nachfolge* (Paderborn: Ferdinand Schöningh, 1964), 9–57.

The Evangelical Counsels in Today's World: "Evangelische Räte in der heutigen Welt?", in *Civitas: Monatsschrift des Schweiz. Studentenvereins*, 21 (1966), 187–97.

Lay Movements in the Church: "Laienbewegungen in der Kirche" (Riflessioni per un lavoro sui movimenti laicali nella Chiesa), in *I Laici e la missione della Chiesa*, ed. Istituto per la trasizione ISTRA (Milan, 1987), 85–106.

OTHER WORKS BY THE AUTHOR ON THE STATE OF THE COUNSELS

Christlicher Stand. Einsiedeln: Johannes Verlag, 1977; 2d ed. 1981. [*The Christian State of Life.* Translated by Mary Frances McCarthy. San Francisco: Ignatius Press, 1983.]

Vorwort zu den Großen Ordensregeln [Foreword to the rules of the great orders]. Menschen der Kirche series, 8:29–98. Einsiedeln: Benziger, 1948; 6th ed., Einsiedeln: Johannes Verlag, 1988.

"Das Ärgernis der Laienorden" [The scandal of the lay orders]. In *Wort und Wahrheit*, 4:485–94. Vienna, 1951.

"Wandlungen im Ordensgedanken" [Changes in the way we think about religious orders]. *Schweizer Rundschau* 52 (Zurich, 1953): 679–84.

"Welt, Orden, Weltorden" [World, orders, and orders in the world]. *Sonnenland: Eine Gabe für Mädchen*, 2d series (1953): 95–97.

"Der Laie in der Kirche". In *«Viel Ämter, ein Geist»: Jubiläumsausgabe der Renaissance.* Edited by Heinrich Nüsse. Einsiedeln: Benziger, 1954. Reprinted in *Sponsa Verbi: Skizzen zur Theologie*, vol. 2, 2d ed. (Einsiedeln: Johannes Verlag, 1971), 332–48. ["The Layman and the Church." In *Explorations in Theology*, vol. 2: *Spouse of the Word*. San Francisco: Ignatius Press, 1991. 315–31.]

"Vom Weltamt der Laien" [On the layman's worldly office]. In *Der Christ in der Welt*, 5:12–15. Vienna, 1955.

"Zur Theologie der Säkularinstitute". *Geist und Leben* 29 (Munich, 1956): 182–205. Reprinted in *Sponsa Verbi: Skizzen zur Theologie*, 2:434–69. 2d ed. Einsiedeln: Johannes Verlag, 1971. ["Toward a Theology of the Secular Institute." In *Explorations in Theology*, vol. 2: *Spouse of the Word*. San Francisco: Ignatius Press, 1991. 421–57.]

"Was hemmt den Nachwuchs an Ordensschwestern?" [What is preventing the growth of religious orders for women?] *Caritas. Zeitschrift für Caritasarbeit und Caritaswissenschaft* 58 (Freiburg im Breisgau, 1957): 217–24.

"Berufung" [Vocation]. In *Zur Pastoral der geistlichen Berufe: Zum Welttag der geistlichen Berufe am 24. April 1966*. Informationszentrum Berufe der Kirche, 3–15. Freiburg, 1966.

"Neue Gemeinschaftsformen in der Kirche" [New forms of community in the Church]. *Universitas. Zeitschrift für Wissenschaft, Kunst und Literatur* 13 (Stuttgart, 1958): 167–74.

"Über den Gehorsam in den Weltgemeinschaften" [On obedience in the secular institutes]. In *Acta II Congressus Internat. Institutorum sæcularium*, 1024–32. Rome, September 20–26, 1971.

"Zur Theologie der Ordensgelübde" [Toward a theology of religious vows]. In *Protokoll der 3. Tagung der Novizenmeister monastischer Gemeinschaften Deutschlands in Engelthal*, 5–14. November 16–20, 1971.

"Nachfolge Christi im Neuen Testament" [The following of Christ in the New Testament]. In *Nachfolge Jesu Christi mitten in der Welt.* Co-authored with Barbara Albrecht, 11–26. Meitingen: Kyrios Verlag, 171.

"Nachfolge Christi in der Liebe—mitten in dieser Welt" [The following of Christ in love—in the midst of this world]. In *Nachfolge Jesu Christi mitten in der Welt.* Co-authored with Barbara Albrecht, 65–79. Meitingen: Kyrios-Verlag, 1971.

"Le Paradoxe des instituts séculiers" [The paradox of secular institutes]. In: *Vie consacrée* 46 (Brussels, 1974): 199–203.

"Göttliches und menschliches im Räteleben nach den Großen Ordensregeln" [The divine and human dimensions of the life of the counsels according to the rules of the great orders]. A lecture given on the Day of Religious Orders in Austria, 1975. *Ordensnachrichten.* Published under the direction of the higher conference of the male religious communities in Austria. Issue number 85 (1975): 394–408.

"Existenz als Sendung: Christus und seine Nachfolge" [Existence as mission: Christ and the *imitatio christi*]. *Schweiz. Kirchenzeitung* 145, No. 48 (December 1, 1977), 705–9.

"Gehorsam im Licht des Evangeliums" [Obedience in the light of the gospel]. *Zur Pastoral der geist lichen Berufe* 16 (1978): 17–27. Reprinted in *Neue Klarstellungen* (Einsiedeln: Johannes Verlag, 1979).

"Berufung—Neutestamentlich" [Vocation in the New Testament]. In *Wirken des Geistes deuten: Hilfen zur Weckung und Förderung geistlicher Berufe*. Edited by the secretary of the German bishops' conference, 12–23. Bonn, 1979.

"Gibt es Laien in der Kirche?" [Are there laypeople in the Church?] *IkZ Communio* 8 (1979): 97–105. Reprinted in *Neue Klarstellungen* (Einsiedeln: Johannes Verlag, 1979), 98–109.

"Wagnis der Säkularinstitute" [The risk of secular institutes]. *IkZ Communio* 10 (1981): 238–45.

"Wer ist ein Laie?" [Who is a layman?]. *IkZ Communio* 14 (1985): 385–91.

OTHER WORKS ON THE SAME THEME

Von Speyr, Adrienne. *Christlicher Stand*. 2d ed. Einsiedeln: Johannes Verlag, 1987. [*The Christian State of Life*. Translated by Mary Frances McCarthy. San Francisco: Ignatius Press, 1986.]

Beyer, Jean, S.J. *Die kirchlichen Urkunden für die Weltgemeinschaften* (Instituta Sæcularia) [The ecclesial documents concerning secular institutes]. Collected by Jean Beyer, S.J., with a foreword by Hans Urs von Balthasar. Der neue Weg series, first volume of the Schriftenreihe für Weltgemeinschaften. Einsiedeln: Johannes Verlag, 1963.

———. *Als Laie Gott geweiht. Theologisches und Kirchenrechtliches zu den Weltgemeinschaften* [Consecrated to God as a layman: theological and canonical considerations in relation to secular institutes]. Translated with an introduction by Hans Urs von Balthasar. Der neue Weg series, vol. 3. Einsiedeln: Johannes Verlag, 1964.

Pollak, Gertrud. *Der Aufbruch der Säkularinstitute und ihr theologischer Ort. Historisch-systematische Studien* [The emergence of secular institutes and their theological position: Historical and systematic studies]. Vallendar-Schönstatt: Patris Verlag, 1986. Especially chapter 6: "Gefüge—Verdeutlichungen aus neuer Gesamtsicht": 1. "Bündelung der Perspektiven in einer exemplarischen Kontroverse zwischen H. U. v. Balthasar und K. Rahner"; 2. "Akzente aus einer neuformulierten Ständetheologie"; Exkurs: "H. U. v. Balthasar als »Theologe der Säkularinstitute« (mit umfassender Bibliographie)". [Syntheses and clarifications from a new perspective: 1. Bringing together perspectives in a paradigmatic controversy between H. U. von Balthasar and K. Rahner; 2. Accents from a newly formulated theology of states of life; Excursus: H. U. von Balthasar as a "theologian of the secular institute," with a comprehensive bibliography.]

INDEX